a beginner's guide to
loom knitting

a beginner's guide to **loom knitting**

easy step-by-step designs for gifts, accessories, and the home

lucy hopping

CICO BOOKS

To my daughter, Francesca Elizabeth Gregg, who in classic style, arrived during the early stages of planning this book.

This edition published in 2026 by CICO Books
An imprint of Ryland Peters & Small Ltd
20–21 Jockey's Fields
London WC1R 4BW
1452 Davis Bugg Road
Warrenton, NC 27589
www.rylandpeters.com
Email: euregulations@rylandpeters.com

First published in 2018 as *Loom Knitting*

10 9 8 7 6 5 4 3 2 1

A CIP record for this book is available from the British Library. US Library of Congress CIP data has been applied for.

ISBN: 978-1-80065-581-2

Printed in China

Editor: Marie Clayton
Designer: Elizabeth Healey
Photographer: Emma Mitchell
Illustrator: Louise Turpin
Templates and illustrations on pages 16–17: Stephen Dew
Stylist: Nel Haynes
Pattern checker: Jemima Bicknell

In-house editor: Anna Galkina
Art director: Sally Powell
Production manager: Gordana Simakovic
Publishing manager: Penny Craig
Publisher: Cindy Richards

The authorised representative in the EEA is
Authorised Rep Compliance Ltd.,
Ground Floor. 71 Lower Baggot Street,
Dublin, D01 P593, Ireland
www.arccompliance.com

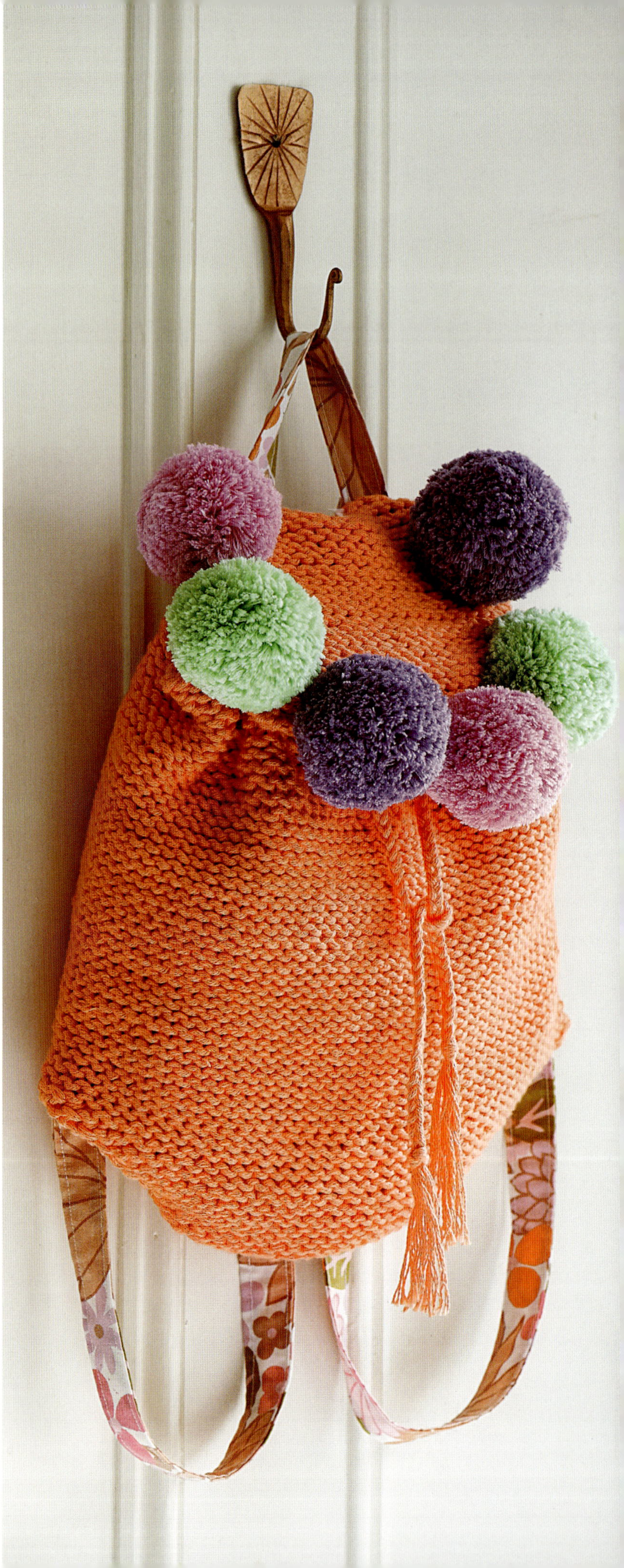

Contents

Introduction

For most of us, an introduction to loom knitting came as a child by using a knitting Nancy or French knitting tool to create meters of narrow tubing to be wound into coasters and placemats. In this book, I hope to inspire you to go bigger and more adventurous with your loom knitting, with 35 exciting projects that use a variety of loom shapes and sizes.

The first chapter, Colorful Accessories and Gifts, has several quick and easy makes that would be ideal as presents. Try making a pineapple charm (page 43), a paper bangle (page 42), or a stylish knotted necklace (page 25). These projects are designed to ease you into the craft, teaching you basics before you make a start on the bigger and more difficult items, such as the patterned ski hat (page 20).

Bags and Cases is a chapter jammed packed full of slightly larger projects that will push your skills further. Here you'll find makes such as a geometric knitted tablet cover (page 62) to keep your tech safe from bumps, or a funky rucksack with pompom details (page 50).

In the third chapter, For Kids, I have created a range of items that are great for children. They will love the jungle finger puppets (page 89) or a funky gem-covered headband (page 84), and there's a beautiful rag doll (page 74) that is sure to become a favorite friend.

The final chapter, Home Accessories, has lots of ideas to brighten up your interior, such as a knitted pouffe (page 116), a retro-style woven throw pillow (page 102), and a chunky basketweave lampshade (page 114).

The wide variety of projects will suit all abilities of craft skill. There is also a clear and concise Techniques section (page 8) to help explain all the stitches, and the cast on and bind (cast) off methods that you will need to make all the items. Now, go grab some yarn, a knitting tool, and a loom and get started on your first loom-knitted item!

Techniques for loom knitting

There are different shapes and sizes of knitting loom available, but there are three main ones for the projects in this book: a round loom with pegs either 3/4in (18mm) or 3/8in (9mm) apart; a long loom with pegs either 3/4in (18mm) or 3/8in (9mm) apart; and a sock loom which has much thinner pegs that are set 1/4in (6mm) apart.

SLIP KNOT

Every project begins with a slip knot.

1 Leaving a 4in (10cm) tail, form a circle with the working yarn.

2 Hold the circle where the yarn crosses and flip it over so that the loop is on top of the working yarn.

3 Pull the working yarn through the circle and tighten as required.

CABLE CAST ON

This creates a neat and firm first row.
You will need a crochet hook for this technique.

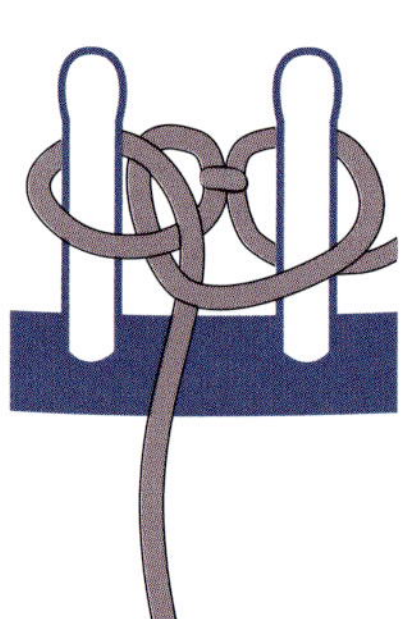

1 Make a slip knot and place on the first peg. Bring the working yarn to the front of the outside of the loom. Using the crochet hook, insert the tip through the slip knot, hook the working yarn around it, and pull back through the slip knot to form a loop. Place on the peg to the left.

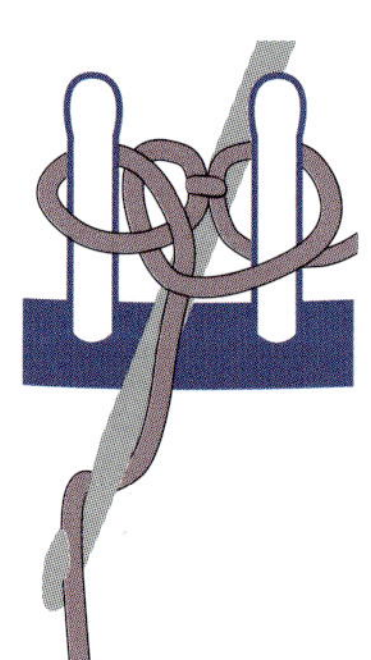

2 Using the crochet hook, take the working yarn between the first and second pegs to the back of the loom. Place this loop on the peg to the left.

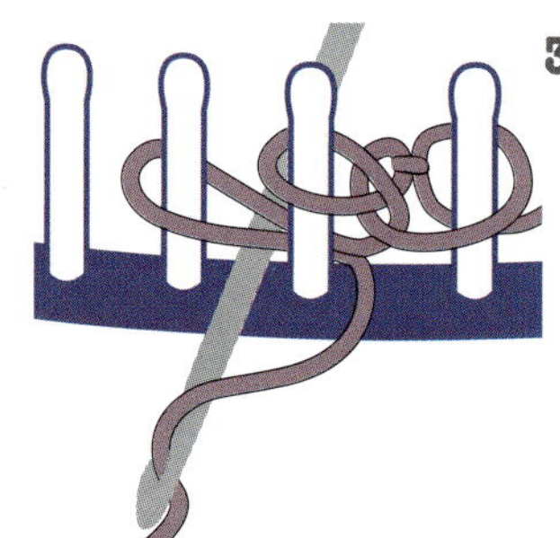

3 Repeat step 2 all around the loom so there are 2 loops on the front of each peg (and 3 on the inside). To complete the cast on, e-wrap the next row, hook the bottom 2 loops over the top one on the peg.

E-WRAP CAST ON

The e-wrap cast on is the easiest method of casting on and creates a fairly loose and flexible first row. It is called an e-wrap because it looks like an "e" when viewed from above.

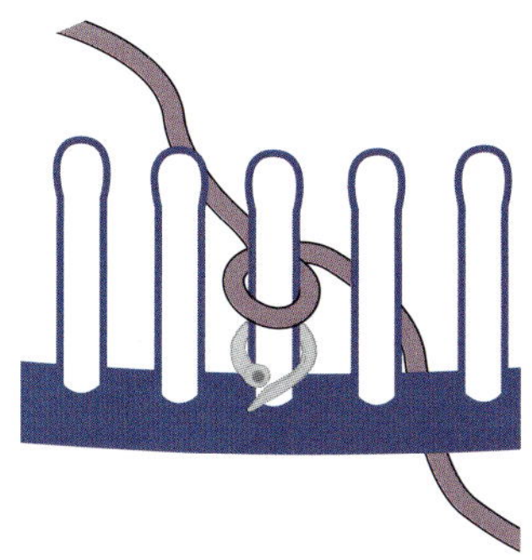

1 Create a slip knot and place it on the first peg of the loom. You can either use the anchor peg, which is the peg on the side of the loom, or choose one on the main loom. Mark with a stitch marker so you know where each row begins.

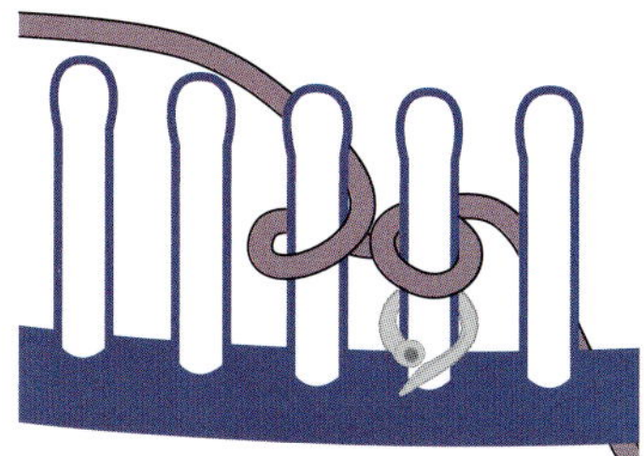

2 Holding the working yarn in your left hand, and with the loom in front of you in your right hand, work in a clockwise direction. Take the working yarn around the back of the peg, and come round to the front and then behind the peg again.

3 Repeat around the whole loom. Be careful to keep the tension even and fairly tight and don't let go of the working end, as your whole row will unravel!

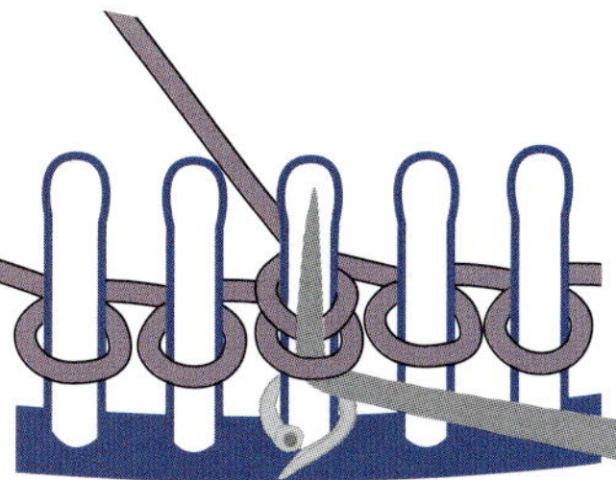

4 Go around the loom a second time, but after each wrap, hook the bottom wrap over the top one using the knitting tool to secure it in place.

5 Repeat all the way around to complete the cast on.

U-WRAP CAST ON

The u-wrap technique is used for flat panels of knitting. Instead of wrapping it around the whole peg, it is just wrapped around the front of the peg.

1 Make a slip knot and place it on the first top peg of the knitting, shown here as peg 1A.

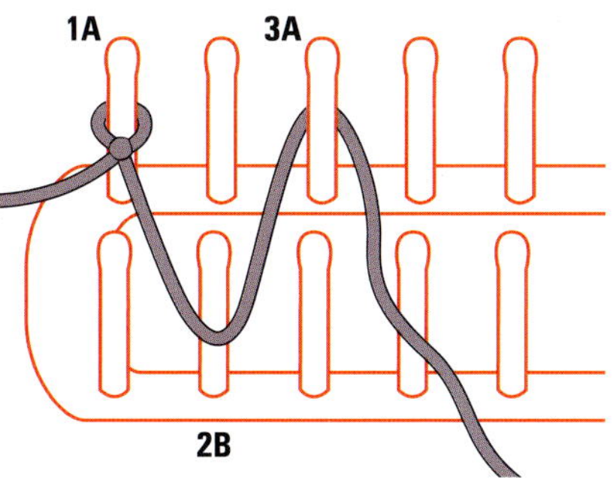

2 Take the working yarn and wrap around the front of peg 2B, then up to peg 3A. Continue in this manner along the board or for the number of stitches you wish to cast on in that color.

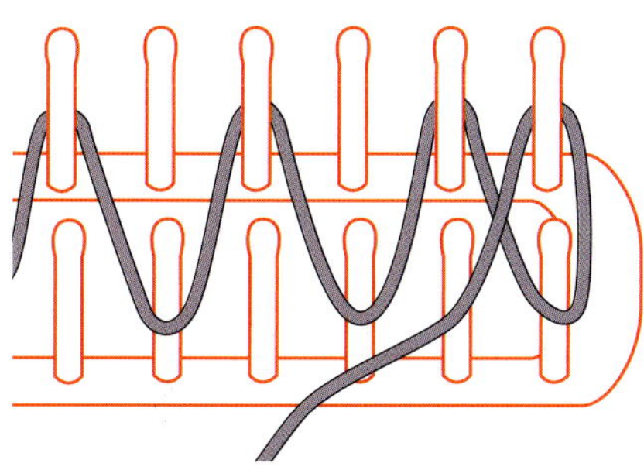

3 To complete, go back along the loom, u-wrapping all the pegs that were skipped in Step 2.

BIND (CAST) OFF

This creates a firm and neat edge that is ideal for most projects.

1 Knit pegs 1 and 2.

2 Move the stitch from peg 2 onto peg 1.

3 Knit the bottom stitch over the top one.

4 Move the stitch on peg 1 onto the empty peg 2.

5 Knit the stitch on peg 3. Now repeat the sequence in steps 2 to 4, so move the stitch on peg 3 onto peg 2, lift the bottom stitch over the top one, then move the stitch on peg 2 onto the empty peg 3.

6 Repeat the sequence along the whole loom. When there is only 1 stitch left, cut the working yarn and thread through this remaining stitch to secure.

GATHER BIND (CAST) OFF

This method creates a gathered/closed end, which is perfect for hats and some types of bags.

1 Cut the working yarn, leaving a 24in (60cm) tail, and thread the tail onto a tapestry needle.

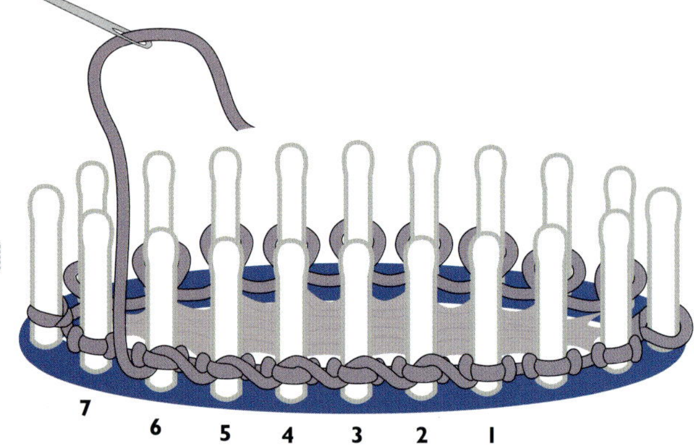

2 Starting on peg 1, thread the needle through the loop and pull through. Repeat around the loom.

3 Gently remove the knitting from the loom and pull the working yarn until the top is closed. Thread the working end through the center hole and work a couple of stitches on the wrong side to secure it in place, then trim the end.

SINGLE CROCHET BIND (CAST) OFF

This technique has a firmer finish than the other bind (cast) off method described. You will require a crochet hook.

1 Remove stitch 1 from its peg and place on the crochet hook.

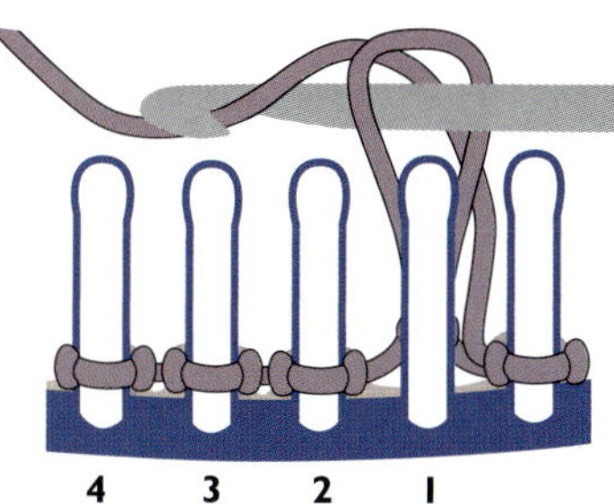

2 Wrap the working yarn around the crochet hook and pull it through the stitch to make a new loop on the hook.

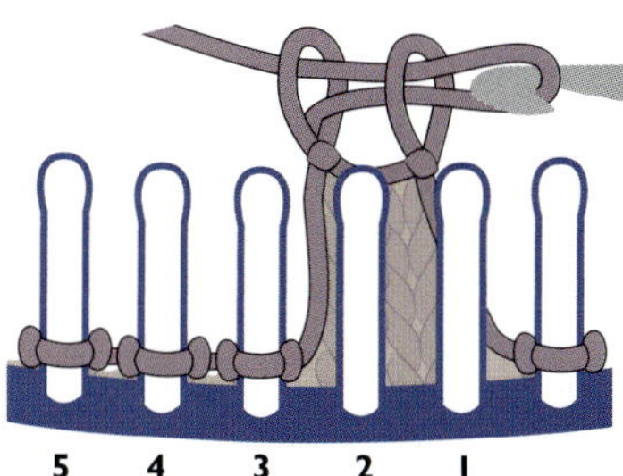

3 Repeat steps 1 and 2 with the stitch on peg 2, pulling the new loop through both the stitch being bound (cast) off and the stitch on the hook.

4 Repeat all the way around until there is only 1 stitch left on the hook. Cut the working yarn to 4in (10cm) and pull through the stitch to secure.

KNIT STITCH (K)

Knit stitch gives the effect of stockinette (stocking) stitch in normal knitting. Each stitch looks like a small V shape on the right side and this is the main stitch used in loom knitting.

1 Lay the working yarn in front and above the stitch on the peg. Insert the knitting tool through the stitch on the peg from the bottom upward.

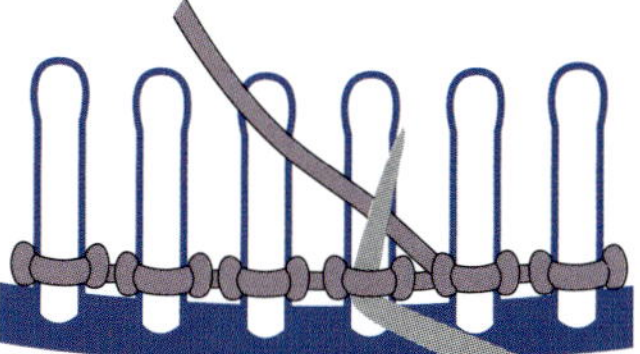

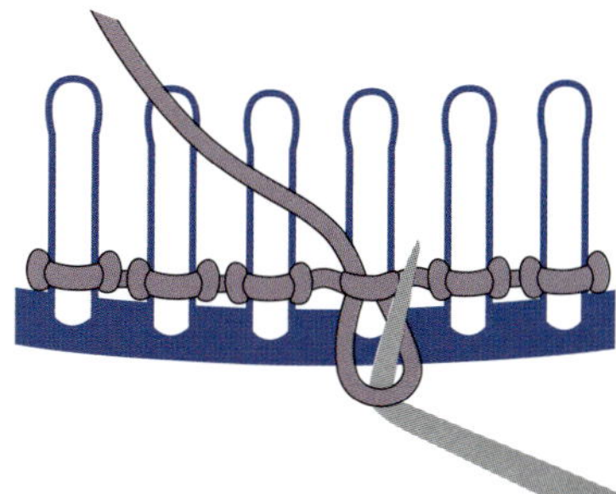

2 Catch the working yarn with your knitting tool and bring a loop through the stitch on the peg.

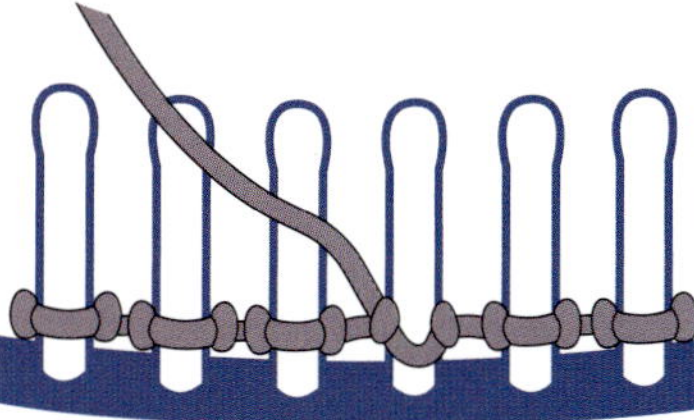

3 Grab the loop with your knitting tool or fingers, pull the original stitch off the peg and replace it with the new one. Pull the working cord slightly to tighten and complete.

E-WRAP KNIT STITCH (OR SINGLE STITCH)

The e-wrap knit stitch uses the same technique as the knit stitch, but instead of laying the working yarn over the peg, you wrap it around the peg before knitting it. This creates a thicker and more stretchy fabric than plain knit.

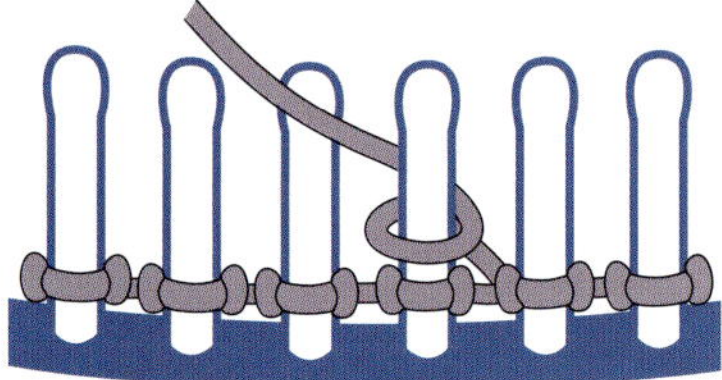

1 E-wrap the peg with the working yarn.

2 Hook the bottom stitch over the top of the peg.

3 Repeat around the loom.

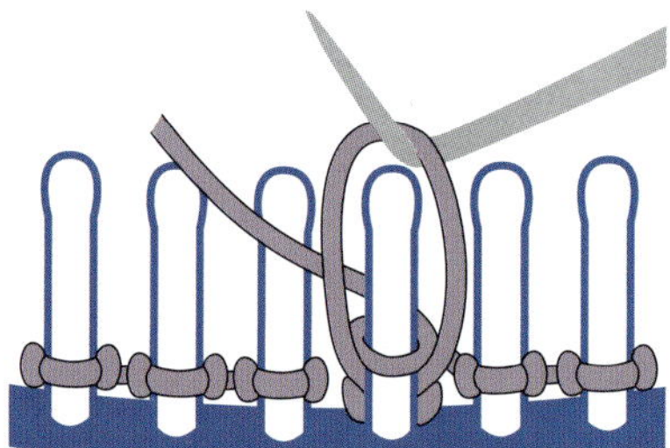

PURL STITCH (P)

This is the opposite of the knit stitch, so each stitch creates a horizontal bump on the right side. It gives the same effect as garter stitch and is also used for ribbing.

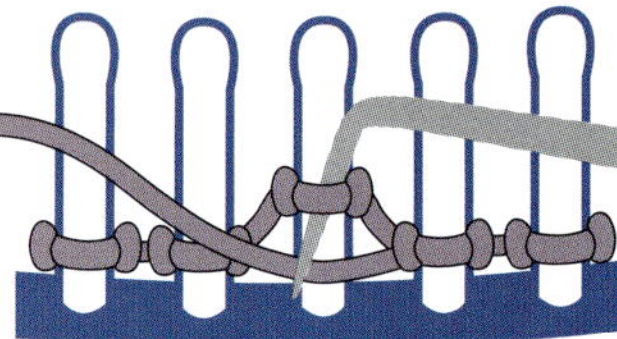

1 Lay the working yarn in front and below the stitch on the peg. Insert the knitting tool through the stitch on the peg from the top downward.

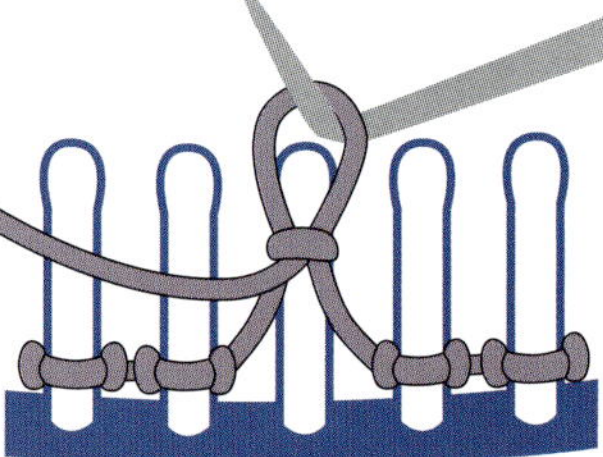

2 Catch the working yarn with your knitting tool and bring a loop through the stitch on the peg.

3 Grab the loop with your knitting tool or fingers, pull the original stitch off the peg and replace it with the new one. Pull the working cord slightly to tighten and complete.

FLAT STITCH

This is similar to a knit stitch, but creates a much tighter finish.

1 Lay the working yarn in front and above the stitch on the peg.

2 Insert your knitting tool through the stitch on the peg from the bottom upward and hook it over the working yarn and off the peg.

FIGURE-EIGHT STITCH

This is a very stretchy and loose stitch. It works up very quickly once you get into the rhythm of the wrapping.

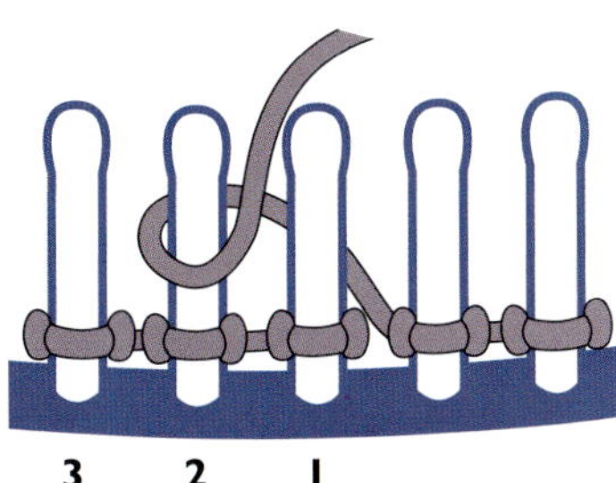

1 Take the working yarn around the back of the first and second peg, then around the front of the second peg.

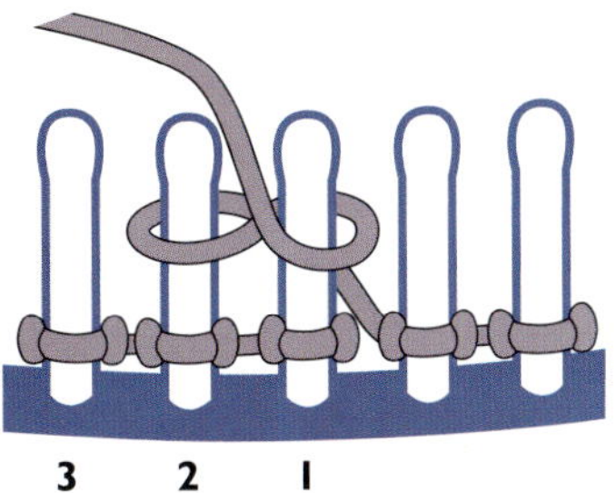

2 Then take it around the back of the first peg, and bring it forward around the front of the first peg.

3 Hook the bottom stitches on the first and second pegs over the wraps just made.

4 Depending on the pattern, you will either repeat the above on the second and third pegs, or on the third and fourth pegs.

ADDING A STITCH

Knitting on a loom can be increased in size as in normal knitting, but you need to make space on the loom by moving the existing stitches over.

1 Move the last stitch on the row outward to the next empty peg (if working in rows), leaving an empty peg within the knitting.

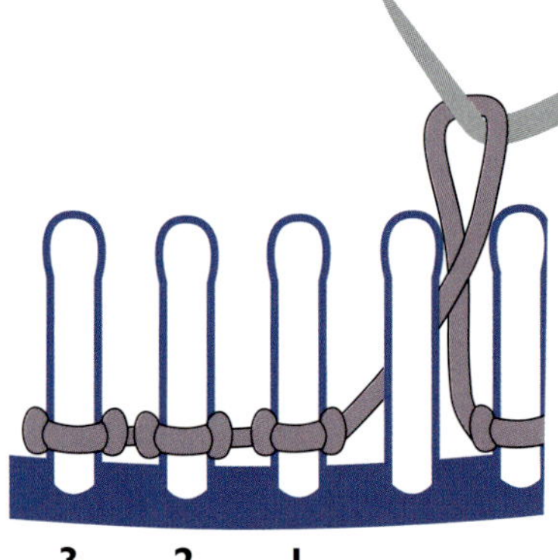

2 With the knitting tool, pick up the bar between stitches, twist it, and place it on the empty peg.

KNITTING 2 STITCHES TOGETHER

This creates a right-slanting decrease and is the easiest way to reduce the number of stitches in your knitting.

1 Move stitch 2 onto peg 3.

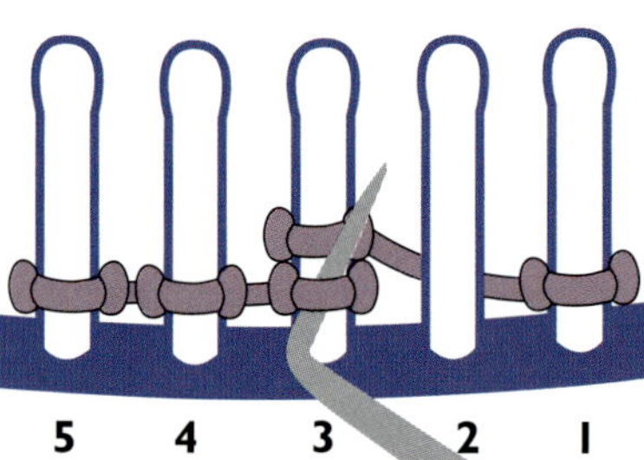

2 Hook stitch 3 over stitch 2.

3 Move the stitches over to close up the gap if the pattern says to do so, to avoid a hole in the project.

SLIP SLIP KNIT

This creates a left slanting decrease.

1 Move stitch 4 onto peg 3.

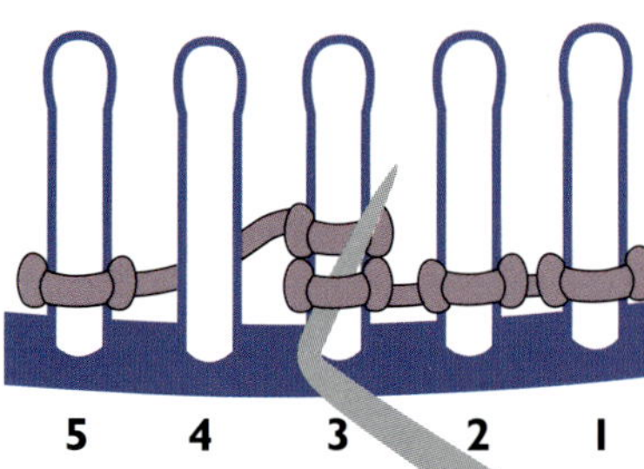

2 Hook stitch 3 over stitch 4.

3 Move the stitches over to close up the gap if the pattern says to do so, to avoid a hole in the project.

WORKING FROM A CHART

Each square of the chart represents a finished stitch. When working in rounds, start in the bottom right corner and work from right to left along the first row of the chart. On the second round, start on the second from bottom row of the pattern, again on the far right, and work right to left.

TWISTING YARNS WHEN CHANGING COLOR

Instead of working with full balls that can get knotted together, cut off lengths of yarn and make mini balls that are easier to work with. When changing yarn colors in the middle of a round or row, the best way to secure them and ensure you do not end up with a hole is to twist them together at the back of the knitting each time you change over.

SINGLE (UK DOUBLE) CROCHET

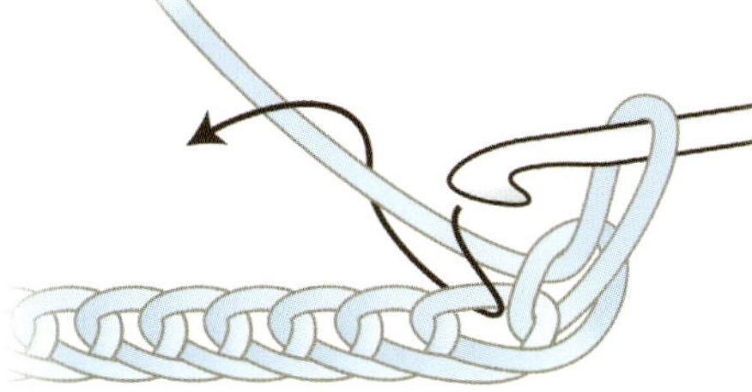

1 Insert the hook into the piece, wrap the yarn over the hook, and pull a loop through the piece only. You'll have 2 loops on your hook.

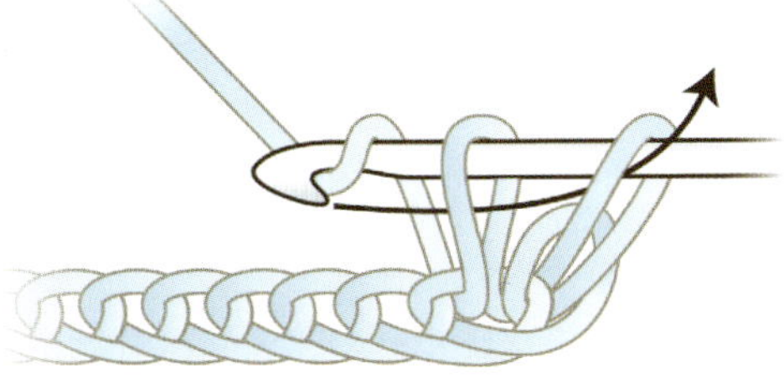

2 Wrap the yarn over the hook again, and pull through the 2 loops on your hook. You'll then have 1 loop left on your hook.

SINGLE (UK DOUBLE) CROCHET SEAM

1 Place the 2 pieces to be seamed wrong sides together. Make a slip knot on your hook and insert the hook through the V at the top of the stitch on both front and back at one end, ensuring you are in the first stitch of both pieces so they line up correctly.

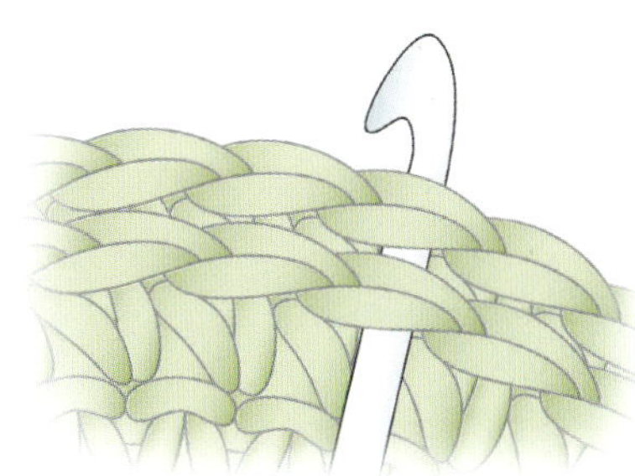

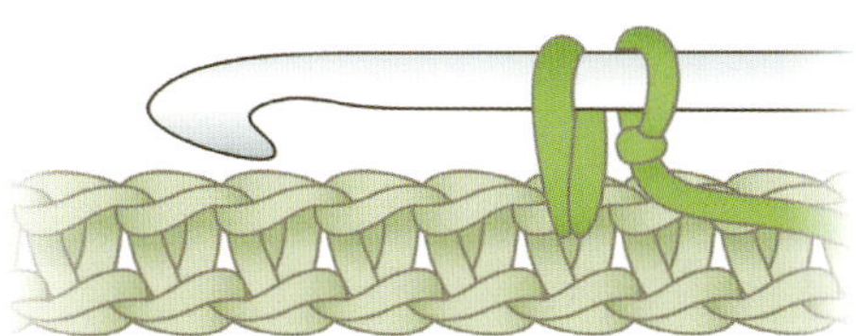

2 Wrap the yarn over the hook and pull through both stitches. You'll have 2 loops on the hook.

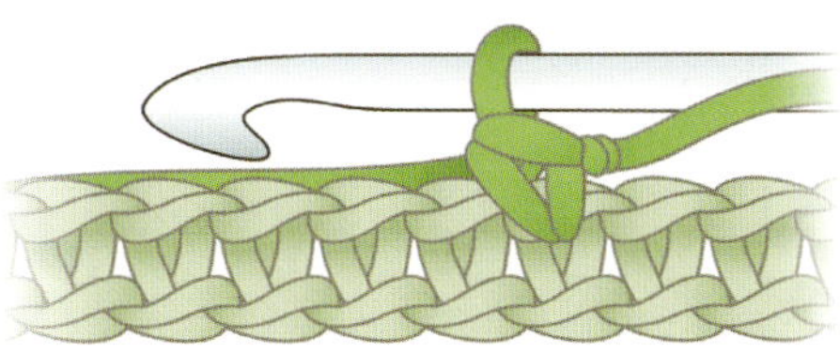

3 Wrap the yarn over the hook again and pull through both loops on the hook to make your first single crochet.

4 Repeat insert the hook through the next pair of stitches, yarn over the hook, pull through both stitches, yarn over hook, and pull through both loops on the hook to the end.

Sewing techniques

RUNNING STITCH

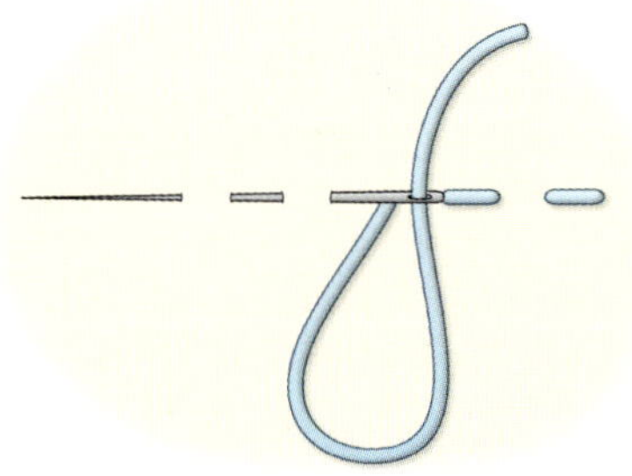

Secure the end of the thread with a few small stitches. Push the needle down through the fabric a stitch length along, and then bring it back up through the fabric another stitch length along. Repeat to form a row of evenly-sized and spaced stitches.

BACKSTITCH

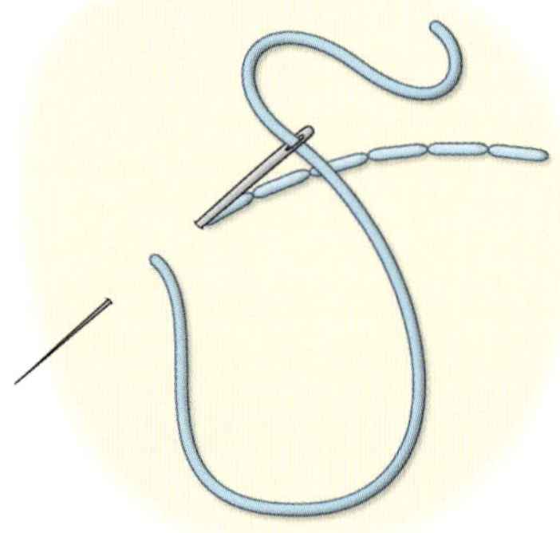

Start as if you were sewing running stitch. Sew one stitch and then bring the needle back up to start the second stitch. This time, instead of going forward, go back and push the needle down through the fabric at the end of your first stitch. Bring it out again a stitch length past where the thread emerges. Keep going to make an even line of stitches that touch each other with no gaps.

FRENCH KNOT

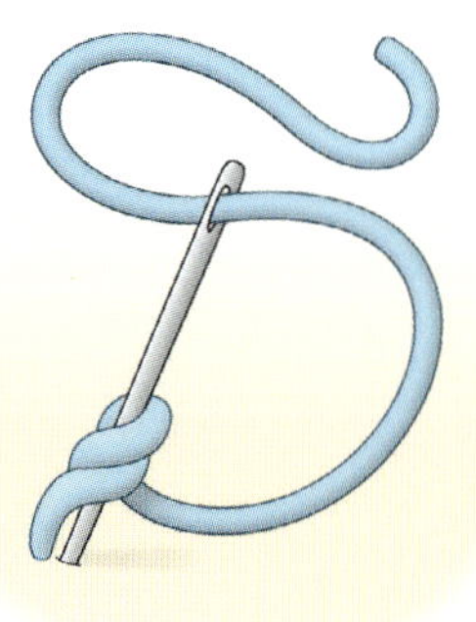

Knot your thread and bring the needle up from the back of the fabric to the front. Wrap the thread once or twice around the tip of the needle, then push the needle back in, right next to the place it came up. As you push the needle in with one hand, hold the wrapped-around threads tightly against the fabric with the thumbnail of your other hand. Pull the needle all the way through. The wraps will form a knot on the surface of the fabric.

BLANKET STITCH

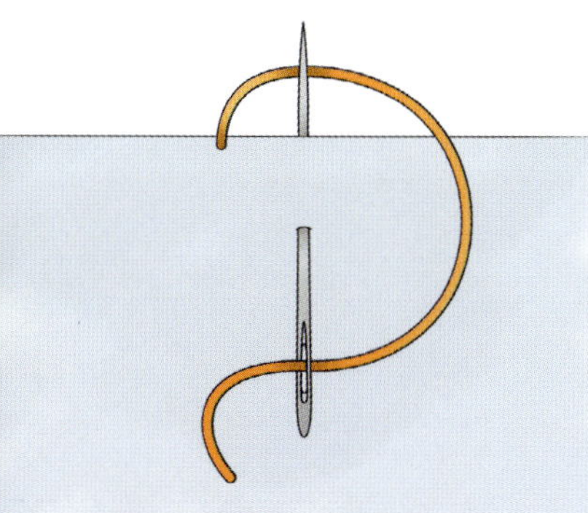

Bring the needle through at the edge of the fabric. Push the needle back through the fabric a short distance in from the edge and a stitch length along, and loop the thread under the needle. Pull the needle and thread through to make the first stitch.

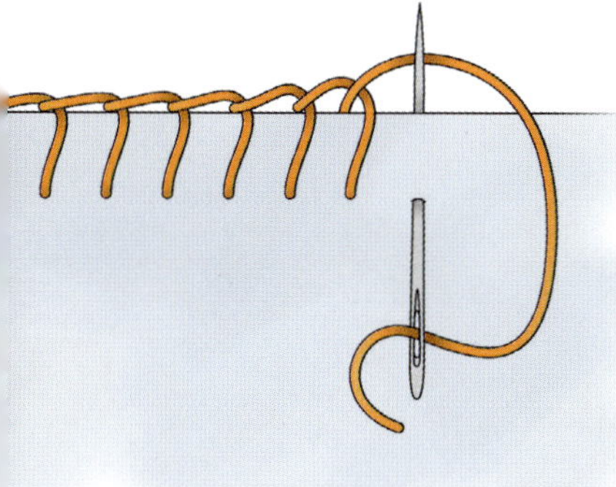

Make another stitch to the right of this and again loop the thread under the needle. Continue along the fabric, and finish with a few small stitches or a knot on the underside.

MAKING POMPOMS

1 Take two cardboard tubes, such as the inners of a paper towel roll, and hold them together. Take the end of a ball of yarn and wrap it over the top of the top tube and between the tubes, then start wrapping around both tubes.

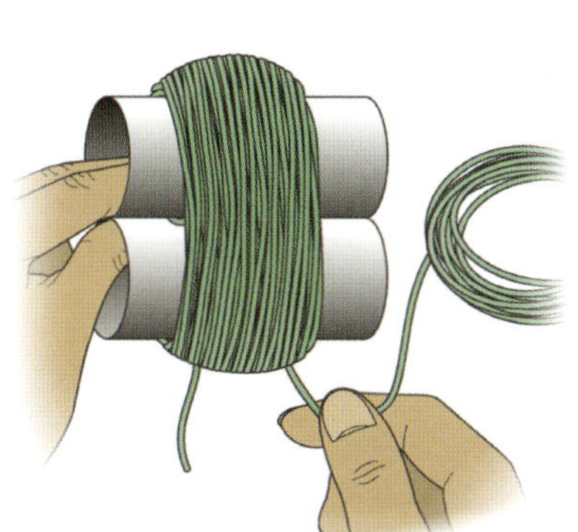

2 Carry on wrapping around both tubes, up to 200 times for a nice, fluffy pompom.

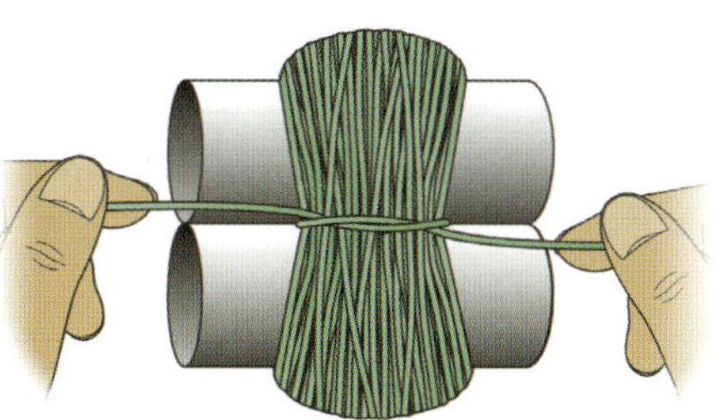

3 Cut the yarn, then cut a separate length of yarn 18in (45cm) long. Slide it between the two tubes and tie the ends.

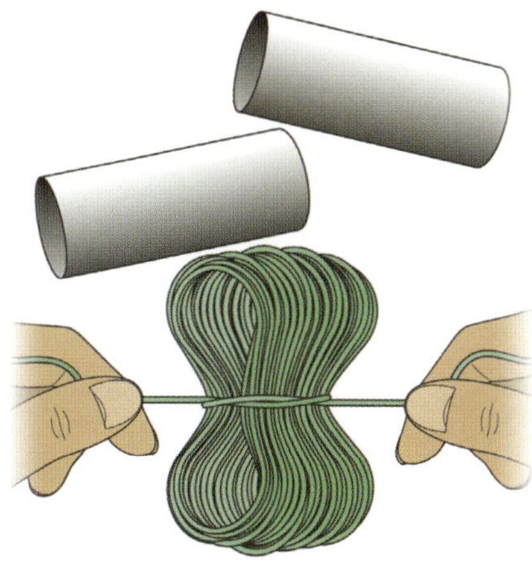

4 Slip the wrapped yarn gently off the tubes. Pull the tie tight, wrap the ends around the center several times, pulling tightly each time, and tie with a double knot to secure.

5 Using sharp scissors, cut through the loops at each end of the wrap. Trim the ends of the pompom until it's thick, fluffy, and round.

CHAPTER ONE

Colorful Accessories and Gifts

Patterned ski hat

This retro-patterned hat is knitted using e-wrap stitches, so the fabric created is super thick and ideal for the slopes. The furry pompom tops it off perfectly!

YOU WILL NEED

- Sirdar Snuggly DK, 55% nylon/ 45% acrylic, light worsted (DK) yarn, 1¾oz (50g) balls, approx. 179yds (165m) per ball: 1 ball each of Soldier Blue 412 (A), Aqua 490 (B), and Cream 303 (C)
- 8½in (22cm) diameter round loom, with 72 pegs set ⅜in (9mm) apart
- Knitting tool
- Scissors
- Tapestry needle
- Blue furry pompom

SIZE

- Standard women's adult size

INSTRUCTIONS

1 Cast on 72 stitches, using Soldier Blue (A) and the e-wrap cast on technique (see page 9).

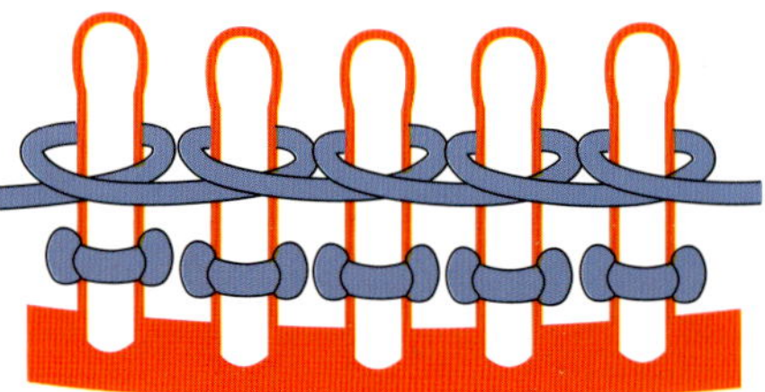

2 Continue using the e-wrap method, and wrap a second round of stitches without hooking them.

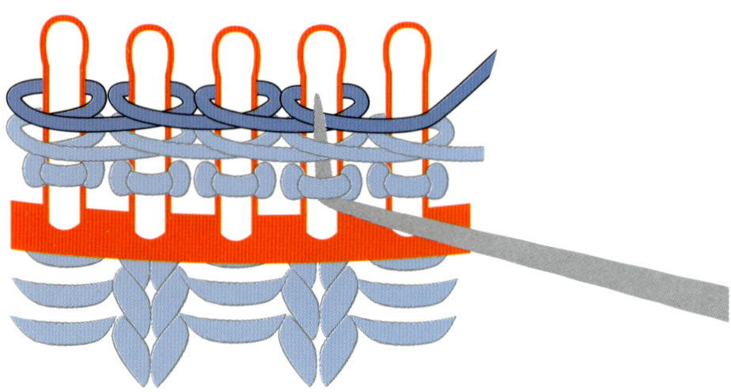

3 On the third round, work k1, p1 around, hooking the bottom 2 stitches over the top one.

4 Repeat steps 2 and 3 for 9 more rounds.

5 Knit for 10 more rounds, continuing to work a round of e-wrap first, then working the round of knit, so that there are always 2 stitches being hooked over the top stitch.

Soldier Blue (A)
Aqua (B)
Cream (C)

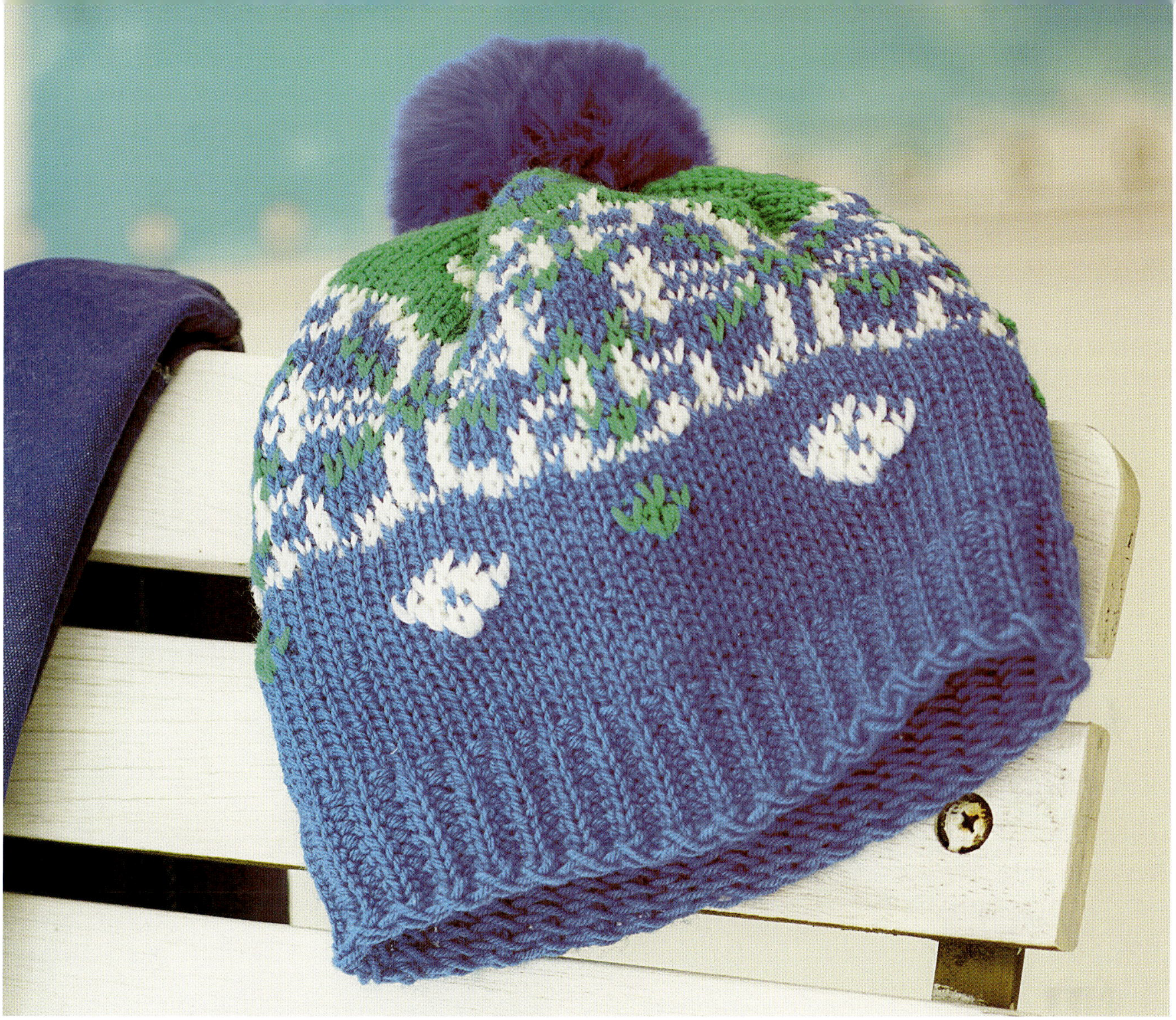

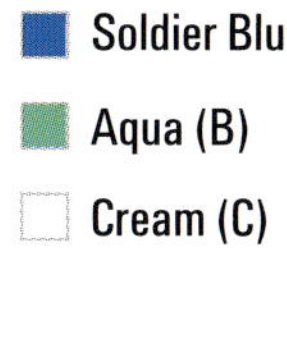

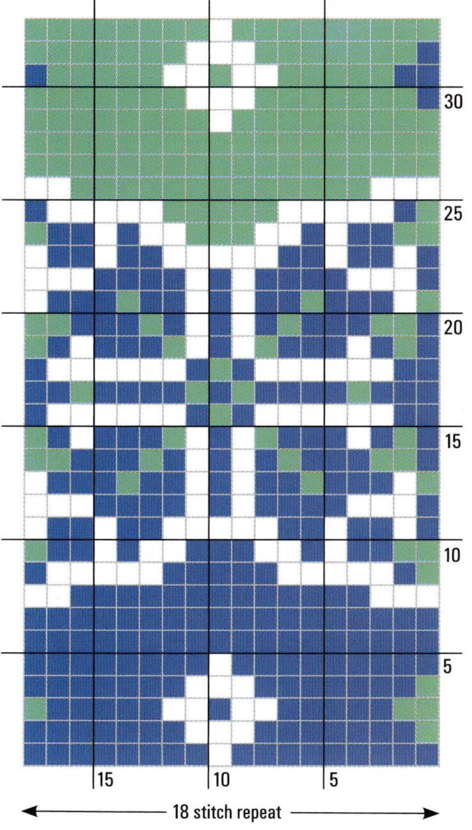

6 Work the pattern from the chart for the next 33 rounds, repeating it a total of four times around the loom, joining in Aqua (B) and Cream (C) as needed. Remember to twist the yarns when changing color, to prevent any holes forming.

7 Knit using Aqua (B) for 4 rounds.

8 Knit 2 stitches together every 9 stitches, so there are 64 stitches left. Knit 2 rounds.
Knit 2 stitches together every 8 stitches, so there are 56 stitches left. Knit 2 rounds.
Knit 2 stitches together every 7 stitches, so there are 48 stitches left. Knit 2 rounds.

9 Work a gather bind (cast) off (see page 10). Use the yarn end from the bind (cast) off to sew on the pompom. Sew in all the loose ends.

Triangle lace scarf

The open knit stitch of this triangular shaped scarf shows off the mohair yarn brilliantly. The perfect scarf for a spring day!

YOU WILL NEED

- Scheepjes Mohair Rhythm, 70% mohair/30% microfiber, laceweight yarn, ⅞oz (25g) balls, approx. 218yds (200m) per ball:
  2 balls of Flamenco 684
- 8½in (22cm) diameter round loom, with 72 pegs set ⅜in (9mm) apart
- Knitting tool
- Scissors
- Tapestry needle

SIZE

- Approx. 55in/140cm at widest point

INSTRUCTIONS

1 Place a slip knot on peg 1.

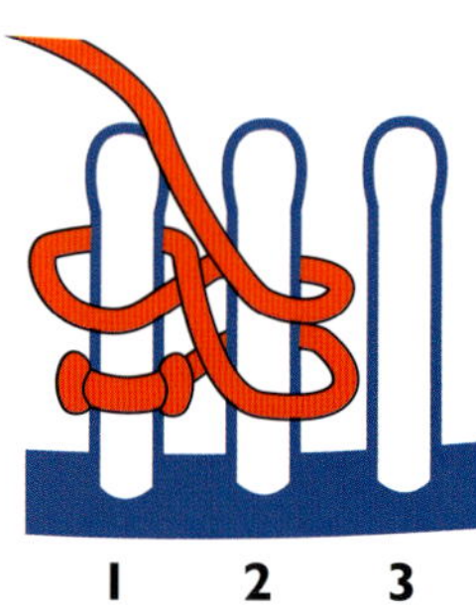

2 Work a figure-eight stitch (see page 13) around pegs 2 and 1 so that there are 2 stitches on each peg, and then hook the bottom stitch over the top one.

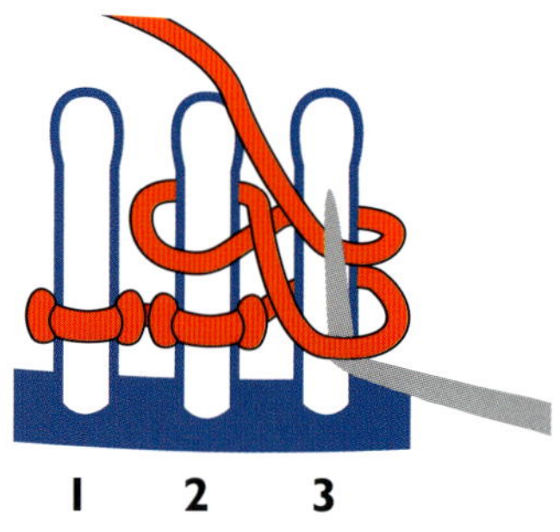

3 Repeat the figure-eight stitch around pegs 3 and 2, and then hook the bottom stitch over the top one.

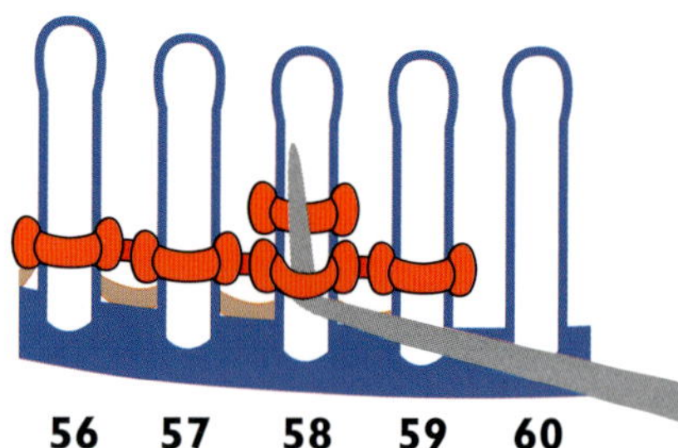

7 To reduce the scarf so that it makes the triangular shape, work a figure-eight stitch on pegs 59 and 60. Then move stitch 59 onto peg 58 and stitch 60 onto the empty peg 59. Hook the bottom stitch on peg 58 over the top one.

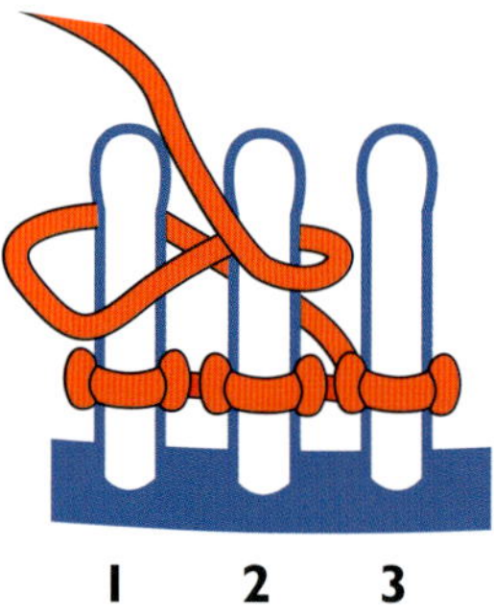

4 Now work figure-eight stitches back from left to right, on pegs 2 and 1. So take the yarn behind peg 2, around peg 1, and then around peg 2. Knit the stitches.

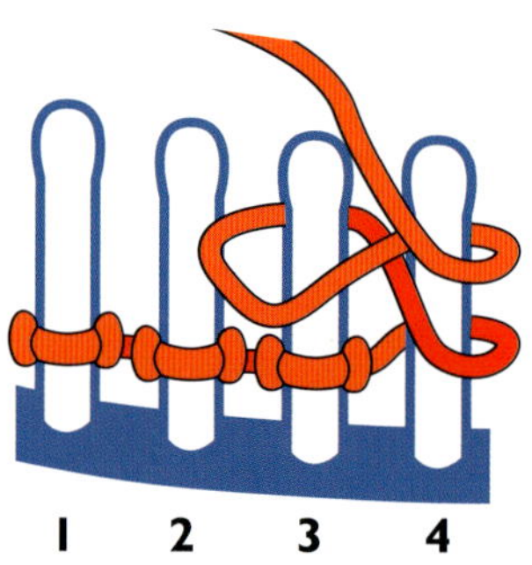

5 Work a figure-eight stitch on pegs 3 and 2, then knit. Work another on pegs 4 and 3.

6 Now work backward again, placing yarn behind peg 4, knitting figure-eight stitch on pegs 3 and 2, then on 2 and 1. Repeat steps 5 to 6, each time increasing the row by 1 peg, until the scarf measures approximately 60 pegs.

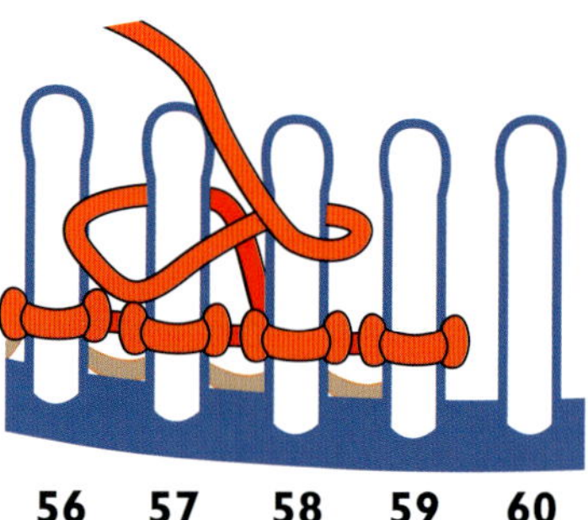

8 Now work figure-eight stitches around each pair of pegs back to peg 1, as you have been doing previously to increase the scarf.

9 Repeat steps 8 and 9 until there is only one stitch left on the loom. Cut the yarn and thread through the last loop to secure. Sew in all the loose ends.

Knotted necklace

Create a stylish necklace from a fine piece of knitted tube, and add silver kumihimo findings to the end for a professional finish.

YOU WILL NEED

- Patons 100% Cotton 4ply, 100% cotton, fingering (4ply) yarn, 3½oz (100g) balls, approx. 360yds (330m) per ball: 1 ball of Pomegranate 1724
- 7¼ x 2in (18 x 5cm) sock loom, with 4 pegs set ¼in (6mm) apart
- Knitting tool
- 2 silver-plated kumihimo ¼in (6mm) cap ends
- Hot glue gun
- Scissors

SIZE

- Approx. 16in/40cm long

INSTRUCTIONS

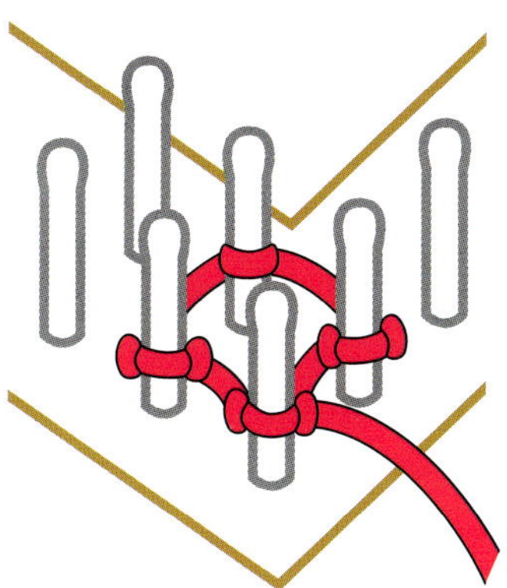

1 Cast on 4 stitches using the e-wrap technique (see page 9).

2 Knit until the piece measures 60in (150cm) long.

3 Work a gather bind (cast) off (see page 10).

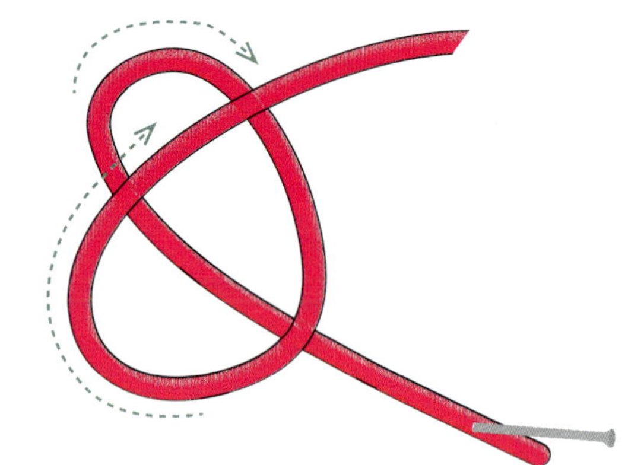

4 Pin one end of the cord to a surface such as the carpet, then loop it around as shown in the illustration.

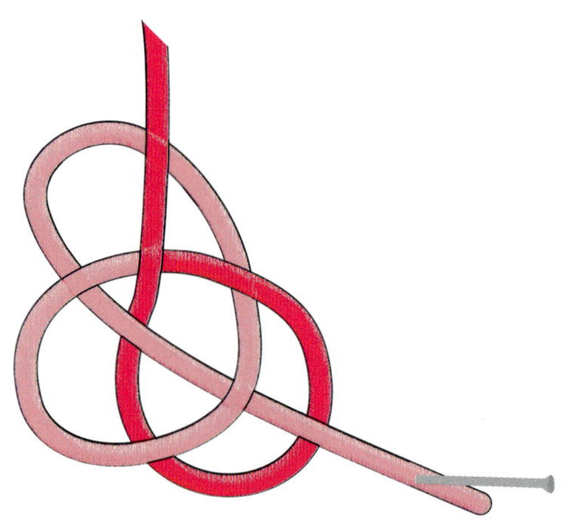

5 Take the cord under the pinned end, under two strands, and over two strands, as shown.

6 Repeat step 4, next to the first knot.

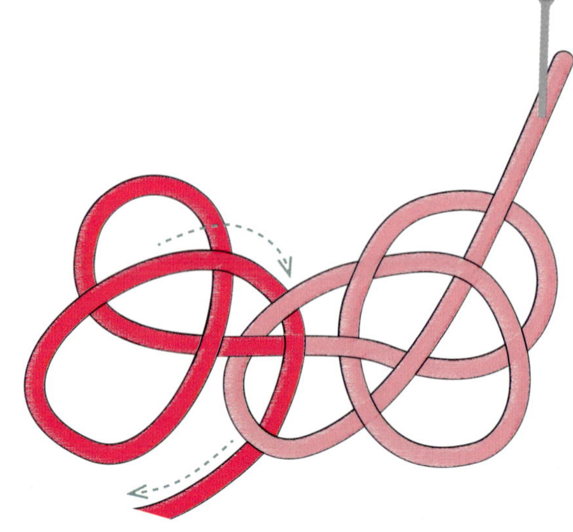

7 Go under, over, and under as shown to link the second knot to the first one.

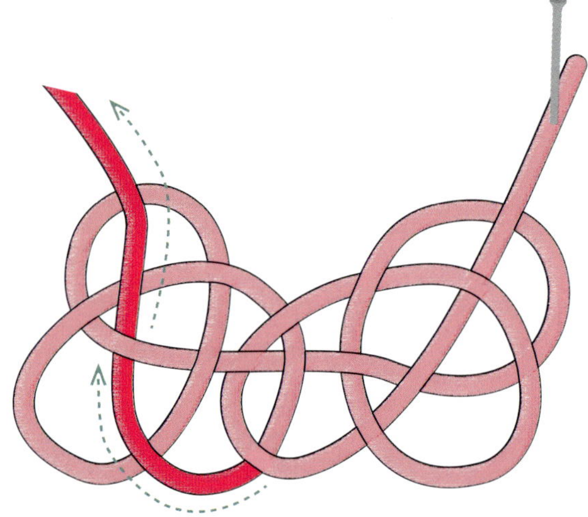

8 Then go over, under, and over two strands of the second knot.

9 Repeat steps 6 to 8 twice next to the knots already formed, and then thread the cord through the last loop. Tighten and neaten so that the knot sits in the center of the cord.

10 Trim the long cords to the desired length, and glue a cap end onto each end.

Infinity scarf

This striking scarf knitted in a bulky yarn is both warm and stylish. It can be worn loose or doubled over for a different look, depending on your outfit or mood.

YOU WILL NEED

- Hobbycraft Women's Institute Soft & Chunky, 70% acrylic/ 30% merino wool, bulky (chunky) yarn, 3½oz (100g) balls, approx. 120yds (110m) per ball:
  2 balls in Black (A)
  1 ball in Heather (B)
- Paintbox Yarns Wool Blend Chunky, 75% acrylic/ 25% wool, bulky (chunky) yarn, 3½oz (100g) balls, approx. 131yds (120m) per ball:
  1 ball in Grape 11 (C)
- 17in (43cm) long knitting loom, with 48 pegs set ¾in (18mm) apart
- Knitting tool
- US size E/4 (3.5mm) crochet hook
- Tapestry needle
- Scissors

SIZE

- Approx. 16in/40cm wide (double this for the total width)

INSTRUCTIONS

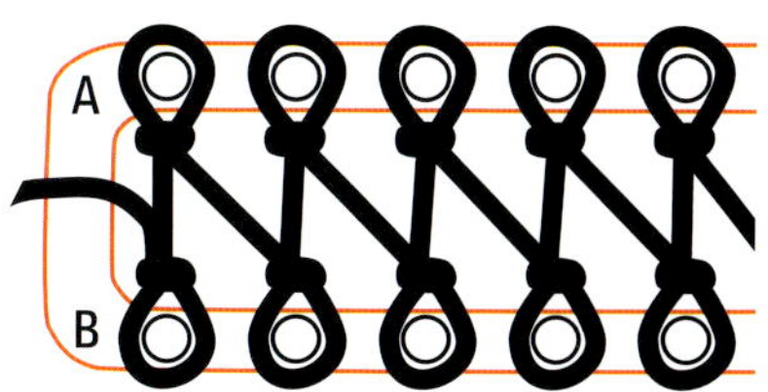

1 Using the Black yarn (A), make a slip knot and place it on bottom left peg 1B. Cast on using the e-wrap technique (see page 9).

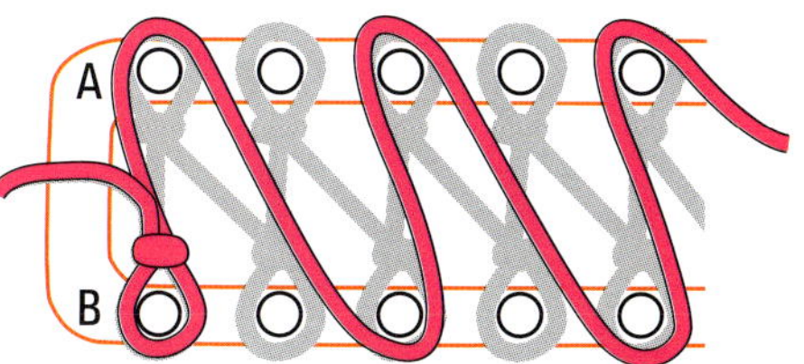

2 Make a slip knot in the Heather yarn (B) and place it on bottom left peg 1B, then use the u-wrap method (see page 9) to wrap every other set of odd-numbered pegs, so over to 1A first, then 3B and 3A, 5B and 5A, and so on along the whole loom.

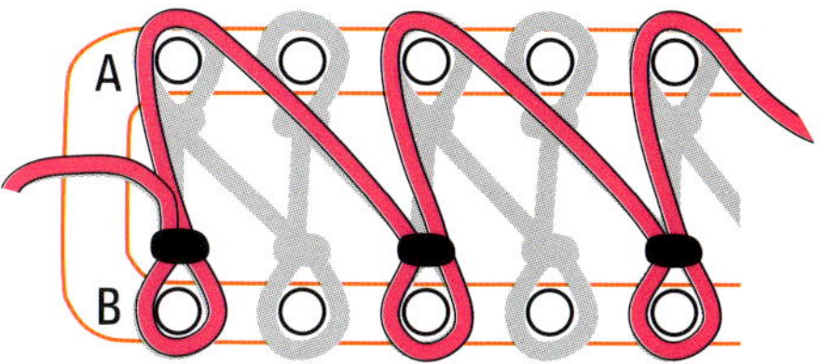

3 Hook the Black (A) loops over the Heather (B) loops on pegs 1B, 3B, 5B, and so on to the end. Do not hook the loops on any of the A pegs yet.

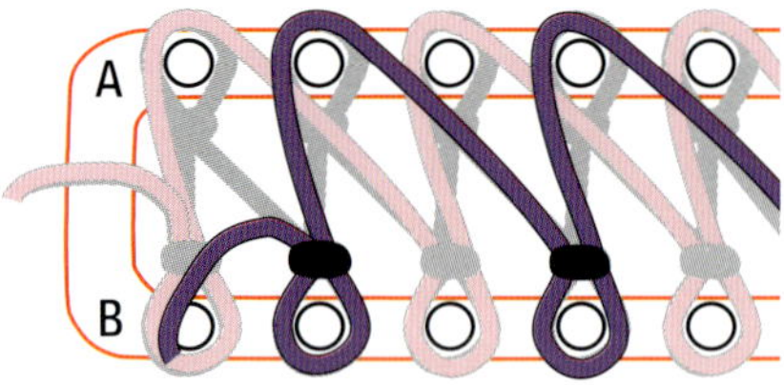

4 Make a slip knot in the Grape yarn (C) and place it on peg 2B, then use the u-wrap method to wrap every other set of even-numbered pegs, so over to 2A first, then 4B and 4A, 6B and 6A, and so on along the whole loom. Hook the Black (A) loops over the Grape (C) loops on pegs 2B, 4B, and so on to the end.

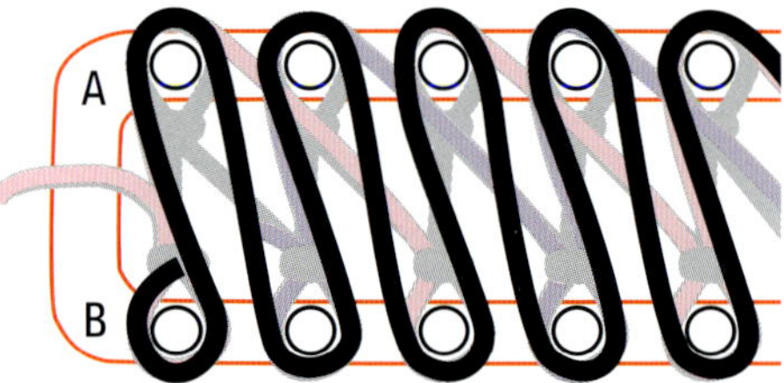

5 Now take the Black yarn (A) again and u-wrap every peg, beginning with 1B.

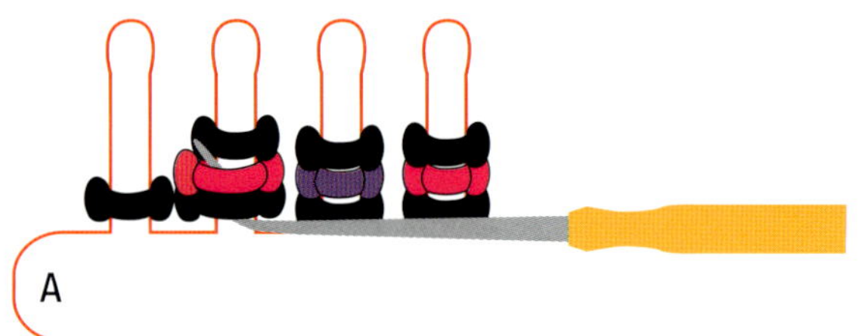

6 Turn the loom around so side A is now closest to you. Hook the bottom two stitches over the top one all along side A.

7 Repeat steps 2 to 4, beginning with a Heather (B) slip knot on the bottom left peg on side A. On the last step you will now be hooking two stitches over each peg on side A, rather than just one stitch.

8 Repeat these alternate rows (steps 2 to 7) until your piece measures 39½in (1m) long.

9 Bind (cast) off using the single (UK double) crochet method (see page 11), leaving a long end. Thread the end into a tapestry needle. Place the two short ends on the scarf with wrong sides together and sew with a backstitch seam (as shown on the right) to create a loop.

10 Sew in all the loose ends to complete.

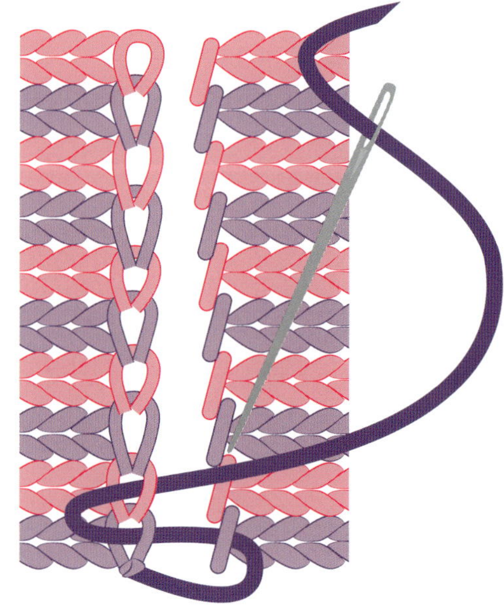

Wave bobble hat

I love the bold, contrasting colors in this funky bobble hat—it would look great in the city or even on the ski slopes! The pompom is a fun extra touch.

YOU WILL NEED

- Rico Creative Cotton Aran, 100% cotton, worsted (Aran) yarn, 1¾oz (50g) balls, approx. 87yds (80m) per ball: 2 balls in each of Mustard 70 (A), Nature 60 (B), and Black 90 (C)
- 8½in (22cm) diameter round loom, with 72 pegs set ⅜in (9mm) apart
- Knitting tool
- 2 cardstock rings, 4in (10cm) diameter with central hole, or 4in (10cm) pompom maker
- Tapestry needle
- Scissors

SIZE

- Standard women's adult size

INSTRUCTIONS

1 Cast on 72 stitches, using 2 strands of Mustard (A) held together and the e-wrap technique (see page 9).

2 Work in k3, p3 rib for 24 rounds.

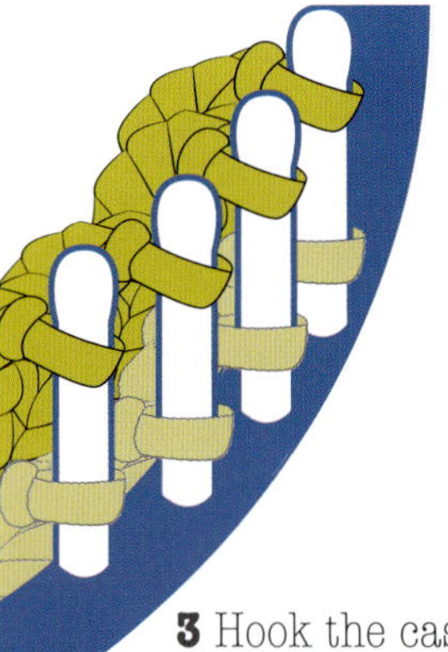

3 Hook the casting-on loops back onto the loom, making sure that they are on their original pegs so the fabric stays straight. This creates a folded double-layer cuff.

4 Hook the bottom loop over the top one on every peg, to join the two edges of the cuff together.

5 Knit for 16 rounds.

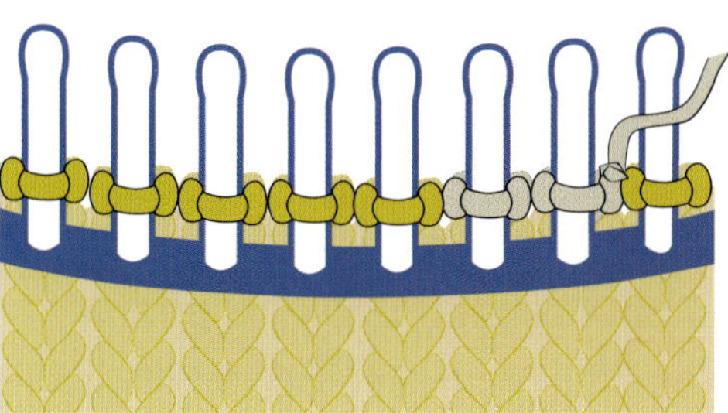

6 On round 41, join in 2 strands of Nature (B). Knit 2 stitches in Mustard (A), 2 stitches in Nature (B), and 4 stitches in Mustard (A)—repeat this sequence all the way around the loom.

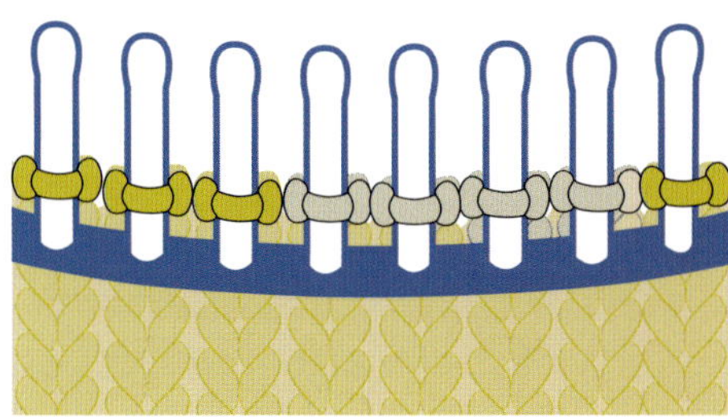

7 On round 42, knit 1 stitch in Mustard (A), 4 stitches in Nature (B), and 3 stitches in Mustard (A)—repeat all around the loom.

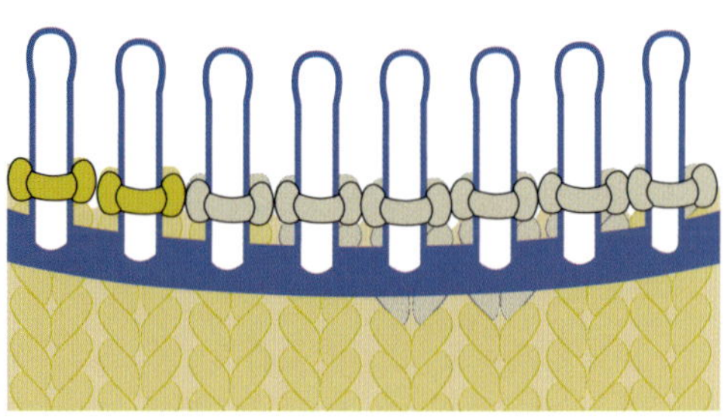

8 On round 43, knit 6 stitches in Nature (B) and 2 stitches in Mustard (A)—repeat all around the loom.

9 Now knit 16 rounds in Nature (B) only.

10 Repeat steps 6 to 8, using Nature (B) in place of Mustard (A) and Black (C) in place of Nature (B).

11 Knit 14 rounds in Black (C) only.

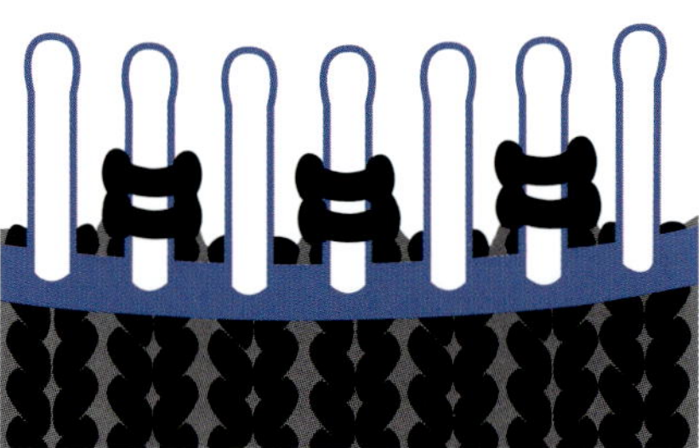

12 Now decrease to shape the top of the hat, by placing alternate stitches onto the adjacent peg, all around the loom.

13 Knit for 2 rounds, knitting each set of 2 stitches as one stitch.

14 Bind (cast) off using the gather bind (cast) off technique (see page 10).

15 Make a pompom (see page 17) using all three colors of yarn. Sew to the top of the hat.

Bow wrist warmers

Before you tackle trying to knit fingers on gloves, try making these pretty bow wrist warmers. They're ideal for keeping your hands warm when you still need to use your fingers to do tasks!

YOU WILL NEED

- Valley Yarns Hawley, 50% cotton/30% silk/20% nylon, light worsted (DK) yarn, 1¾oz (50g) balls, approx. 135yds (123m) per ball: 1 ball each of Basil 14 (A), Blue Skies 06 (B), and Amethyst Dust 11 (C)
- 7¼ x 2in (18 x 5cm) sock loom, with 34 pegs set ¼in (6mm) apart
- US size G/6 (4mm) crochet hook
- Knitting tool
- Tapestry needle
- Scissors

SIZE

- Standard women's adult size (approx. 10in/25cm long)

INSTRUCTIONS

1 Using Basil (A), cast on 34 stitches using the cable cast on technique (see page 8).

2 For the first round, k1, p1 all around the loom. Repeat until you've worked 20 rounds.

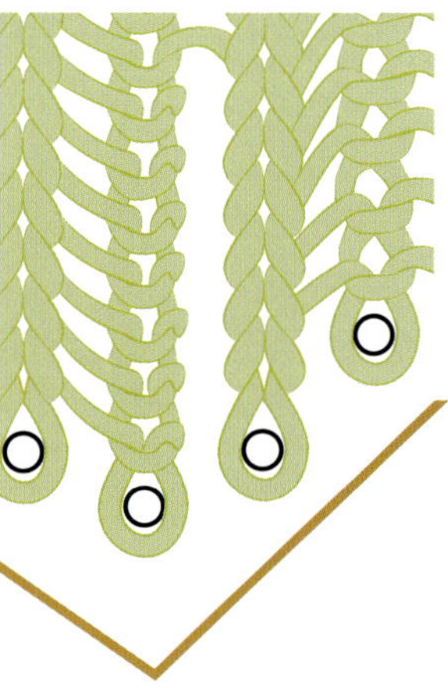

3 Now create the thumb slit by working backward and forward in rows between the first and last stitch of the round, instead of working in the round. Work 16 rows in k1, p1 ribbing throughout.

4 Now begin to work in the round again, to complete the top of the wrist warmer.

5 Change to Blue Skies (B) and work k1, p1 rib for 6 rounds.

6 Change to Basil (A) and work k1, p1 rib for 6 rounds.

7 Repeat steps 5 and 6 three more times, until there are four Blue Skies (B) stripes and four Basil (A) stripes.

8 Bind (cast) off, and sew in all the loose ends.

9 Set the loom to 22 stitches. Using Amethyst Dust (C), cast on using the cable cast on method. Work flat stitch (see page 13) for 12 rows.

10 Bind (cast) off, leaving an 8in (20cm) yarn end. Wrap the yarn end around the center of the knitting a few times to create a bow, and then weave the yarn end through the wraps once or twice to secure, using the tapestry needle.

11 Use the remaining yarn end to sew the bow to the front of your wrist warmer.

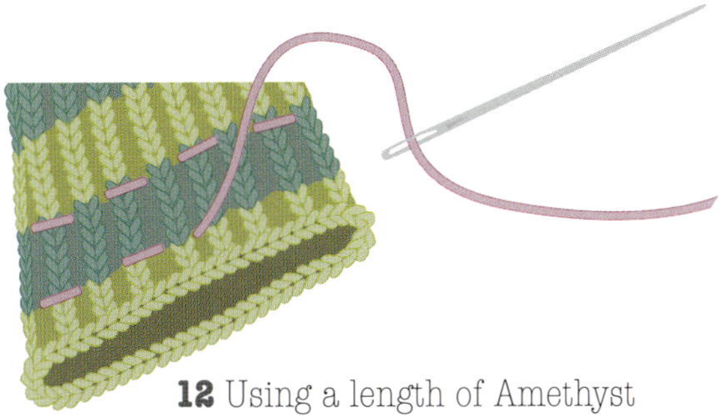

12 Using a length of Amethyst Dust (C) in the needle, work running stitch (see page 16) along either side of the Blue Skies (B) stripe at the bottom of the mitten.

13 Repeat all the steps to make a second wrist warmer. Make sure you sew the bow to the opposite side of the mitten this time, so you have a pair!

Lace trim boot cuffs

Combine a rustic wool yarn with a delicate lace trim in these cozy boot cuffs. Perfect to wear under rubber boots or with walking shoes on a day out in the country. Make sure to use the yarn doubled throughout.

YOU WILL NEED

- Cascade 220 Superwash, 100% wool, light worsted (DK) yarn, 3½oz (100g) balls, approx. 219yds (200m) per ball: 2 balls of Faded Rose 364
- 8½in (22cm) diameter round loom, with 24 pegs set ¾in (18mm) apart
- Knitting tool
- US size E/4 (3.5mm) crochet hook
- Tapestry needle
- 40in (1m) of cream lace
- Sewing needle and cream thread
- Scissors

SIZE

- Approx. 8in (20cm) long

INSTRUCTIONS

1 Using two strands of yarn together for a chunky effect, make a slip knot and place on the first peg of the loom.

2 Using the e-wrap technique (see page 9), cast on 24 stitches.

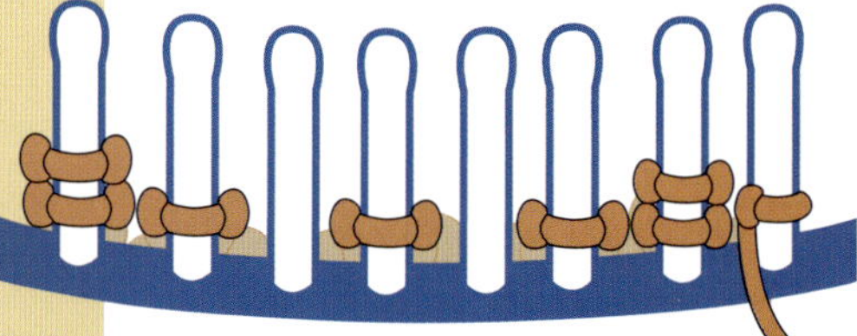

3 For round 1, knit the first stitch, lift stitch 2, place the stitch on peg 3 onto peg 2 and then replace stitch 2, move stitch 4 to peg 3. Knit peg 5. Lift stitch 8, place the stitch on peg 7 onto peg 8 and then replace stitch 8, and move stitch 6 onto peg 7. Treat the 2 stitches on pegs 2 and 8 as one stitch when knitting, and e-wrap the empty pegs 4 and 6. Repeat this sequence of moves twice more to complete the round.

4 Knit round 2.

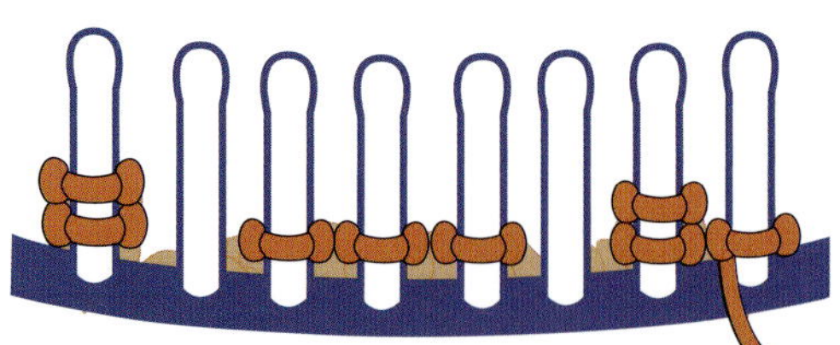

5 For round 3, knit the first stitch, lift stitch 2, place the stitch on peg 3 onto peg 2 and then replace stitch 2. Knit pegs 4, 5, and 6. Lift stitch 8, place the stitch on peg 7 onto peg 8, and replace stitch 8. Treat the 2 stitches on pegs 2 and 8 as one stitch when knitting, and e-wrap the empty pegs 3 and 7. Repeat this sequence of moves twice more to complete the round.

6 Knit round 4.

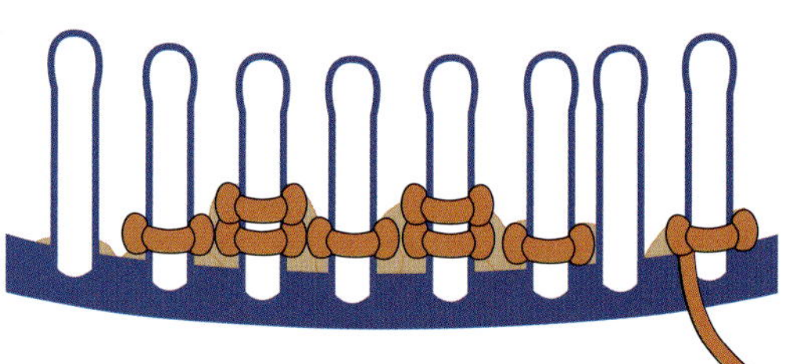

7 For round 5, knit the first stitch, lift stitch 4, place the stitch on peg 3 onto peg 4, and then replace stitch 4, move stitch 2 to peg 3. Knit peg 5. Lift stitch 6, place the stitch on peg 7 onto peg 6, and then replace stitch 6, and move stitch 8 onto peg 7. Treat the 2 stitches on pegs 4 and 6 as one stitch when knitting, and e-wrap the empty pegs 2 and 8. Repeat this sequence of moves twice more to complete the round.

8 Knit round 6.

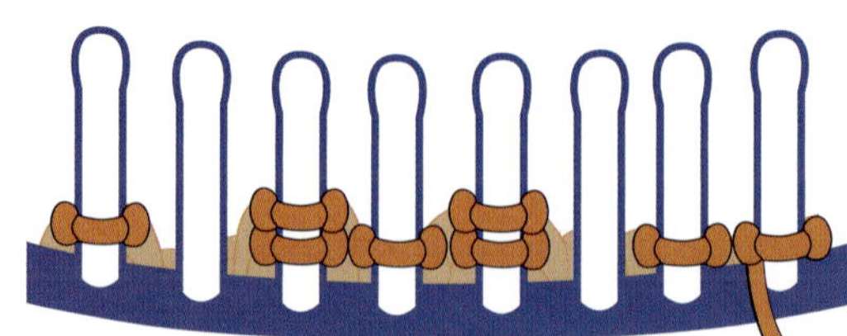

9 For round 7, knit the first 2 stitches, lift stitch 4, place the stitch on peg 3 onto peg 4, and then replace stitch 4. Knit peg 5. Lift stitch 6, place the stitch on peg 7 onto peg 6l and then replace stitch 6. Treat the 2 stitches on pegs 4 and 6 as one stitch when knitting, and e-wrap the empty pegs 3 and 7. Repeat this sequence of moves twice more to complete the round.

10 Work 1 knit round, then repeat steps 3 to 9 five times. Bind (cast) off using the single (UK double) crochet method (see page 11).

11 Sew in the loose ends using the tapestry needle.

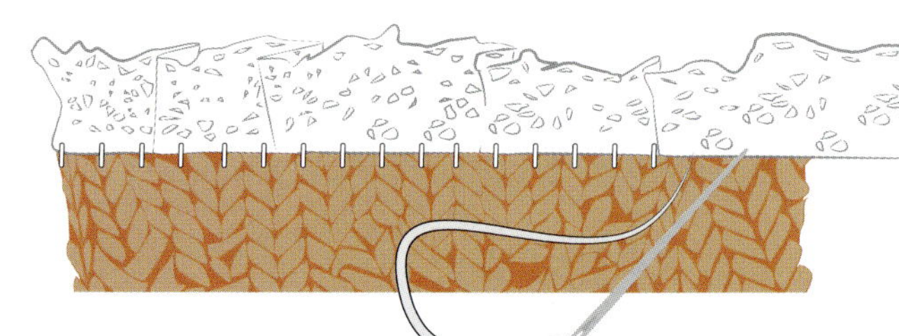

12 Cut the lace so that it is slightly longer than the circumference of your cuff and pin to the top of the cuff, pleating as necessary to fit and to allow for stretch. Overlap the ends. Sew in place using the sewing thread.

13 Repeat all the steps to make the second cuff.

Colorblock mittens

These gorgeous mittens will keep your hands toasty warm on chilly days and add a pop of color.

YOU WILL NEED

- Rico Essential Merino DK, 100% merino, light worsted (DK) yarn, 1¾oz (50g) balls, approx. 131yds (120m) per ball: 1 ball each of Grey 24 (A), Green 42 (B), and Yellow 65 (C)
- 7¼ x 2in (18 x 5cm) sock loom, with 50 pegs set ¼in (6mm) apart
- Knitting tool
- Scissors
- Tapestry needle

SIZE

- Standard women's adult size

INSTRUCTIONS

1 Cast on 30 stitches in the round at one end of the loom, using Grey (A) and the e-wrap technique (see page 9).

2 Work in k1, p1 rib for 35 rounds, and then knit 1 round.

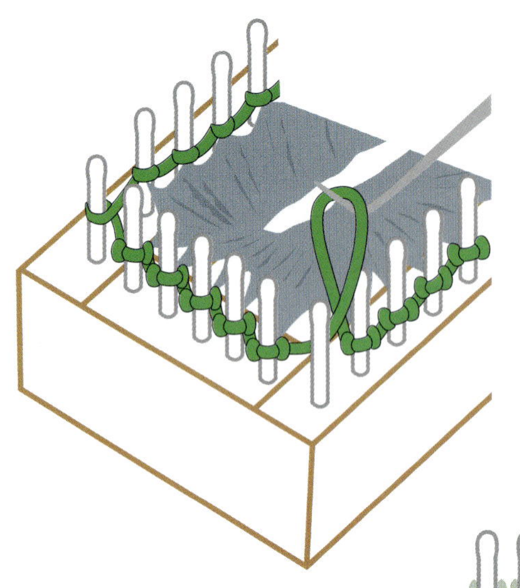

3 Move all the stitches on each long side down by one peg, so you have a spare peg in each corner. Change to Green (B) and increase by 4 stitches, so working on one more peg at each corner of the loom. You'll have 34 stitches.

TIP

Although it's a bit fiddly, it's best to move the stitches down in step 3 so that your increases are evenly spaced around the mittens.

4 Knit for 2 rounds.

5 Still working in Green (B), repeat steps 3 and 4 three more times, so you will finish with 46 stitches on the loom.

6 Knit for 9 rounds.

7 Thread the first 7 stitches on the loom onto a piece of waste yarn and remove them. E-wrap the empty pegs and knit the rest of the round.

8 Knit another 35 rounds in Green (B).

9 Change to Yellow (C), and work seed (moss) stitch (first round: k1, p1, second round: p1, k1) for 30 rounds.

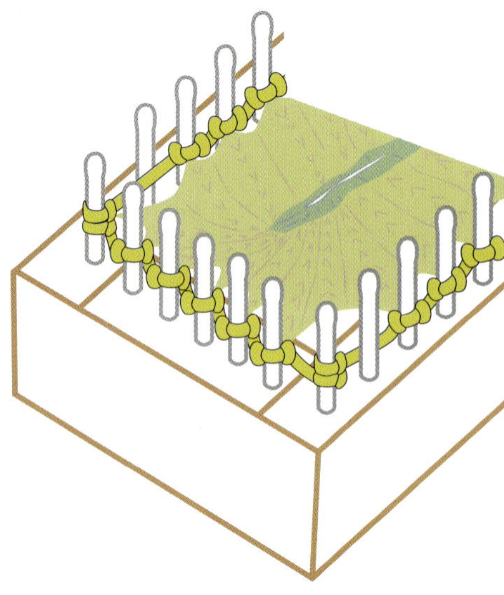

10 Decrease by 4 stitches, so move one stitch at each corner onto the adjacent peg so you can set the loom to 42 stitches.

11 Knit 2 rounds.

12 Repeat steps 10 and 11 three more times until there are only 30 stitches left on the loom.

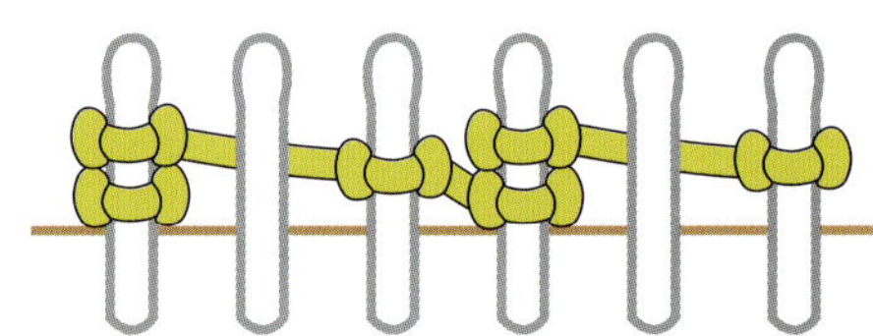

13 Then decrease by 10 stitches, so place 2 stitches on one peg, skip a peg, then place 2 stitches on the next peg and so on, until you have reduced the loom down to 20 stitches.

14 Work a gather bind (cast) off (see page 10), and then sew in all the loose ends. Repeat all the steps to make a second mitten.

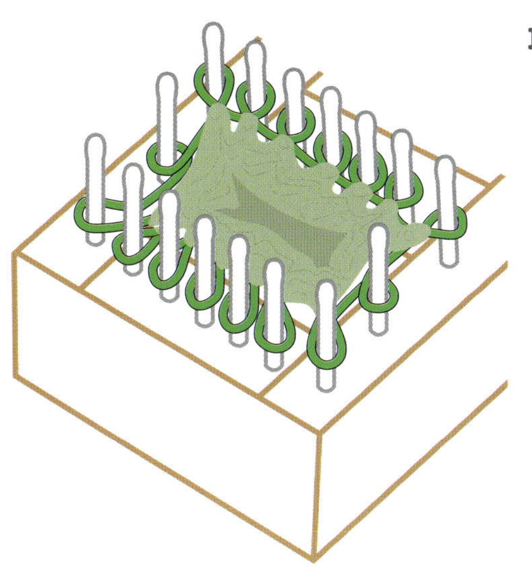

15 To make the thumb, set your loom to 16 pegs. Place the 7 stitches left on the waste yarn in step 7 onto pegs 1 to 7, then place the e-wrapped stitches on pegs 9 to 15. To prevent any gaps in the thumb join, pick up one cross bar stitch from each side and place those on pegs 8 and 16.

16 Attach Green (B) to peg 1 and knit for 4in (10cm), or for desired thumb length. Work a gather bind (cast) off, sew in the loose ends, and repeat with the other mitten.

Paper bangles

Create these stylish chunky bangles using paper twine. Make several and layer them up for a cool look.

YOU WILL NEED

- 27½yds (25m) of ⅛in (3mm) diameter paper raffia in each of pink and turquoise
- 2in (5cm) diameter round loom, with 8 pegs set ⅜in (9mm) apart
- Knitting tool
- Scissors
- Tapestry needle

SIZE

- Approx. 4in (10cm) diameter

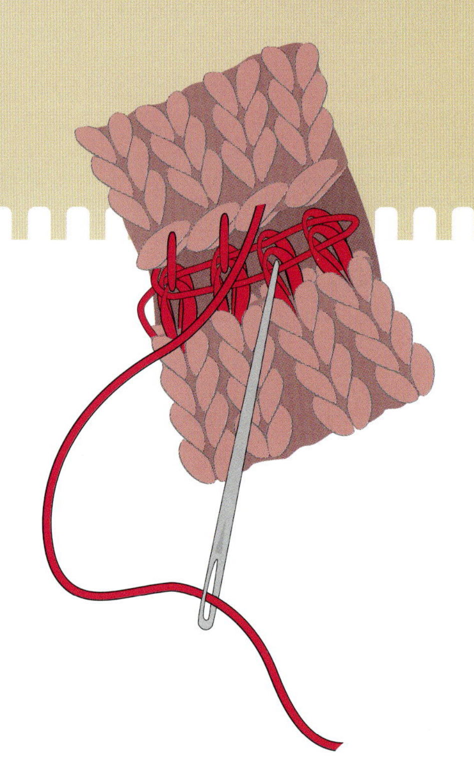

INSTRUCTIONS

1 Using pink, cast on 8 stitches using the e-wrap technique (see page 9).

2 Knit until the tube measures 10–11in (25–28cm) long, depending on your wrist size.

3 Gather bind (cast) off (see page 10), leaving a long end.

4 Using the long end, sew the ends of the tube together neatly to create a bangle.

5 Repeat with the turquoise raffia, but work in purl.

Pineapple charm

Add a tropical feel to your keys or purse, with this bobble knitted pineapple charm!

YOU WILL NEED

- Drops Paris, 100% cotton, worsted (Aran) yarn, 1¾oz (50g), approx. 82yds (75m) per ball: 1 ball of Mustard 41
- 7¼ x 2in (18 x 5cm) sock loom, with 20 pegs set ¼in (6mm) apart
- Knitting tool
- Scissors
- Tapestry needle
- Sewing needle and green thread
- Stuffing
- 9 x 3in (22.5 x 7.5cm) strip of green felt
- Key ring/bag charm attachment

SIZE

- Approx. 2¼in (6cm) tall

INSTRUCTIONS

1 Cast on 20 stitches using the e-wrap technique (see page 9). Knit 1 round.

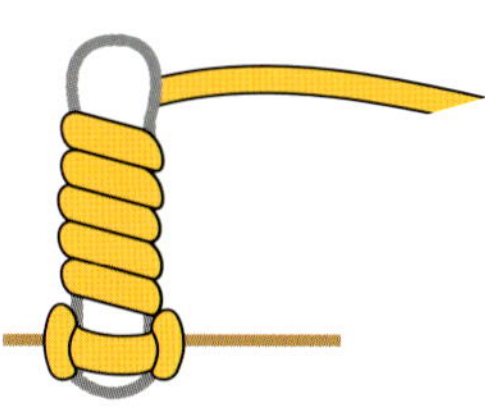

2 K1, and then begin to work a bobble on peg 2 by wrapping the yarn around the peg 5 times.

3 Hook the bottom stitch over the 5 wraps.

4 Then hook the bottom wrap over the 4 remaining wraps.

5 Repeat step 4 but over 3 wraps, then 2 wraps, and finally 1 wrap so there is only one stitch on the peg.

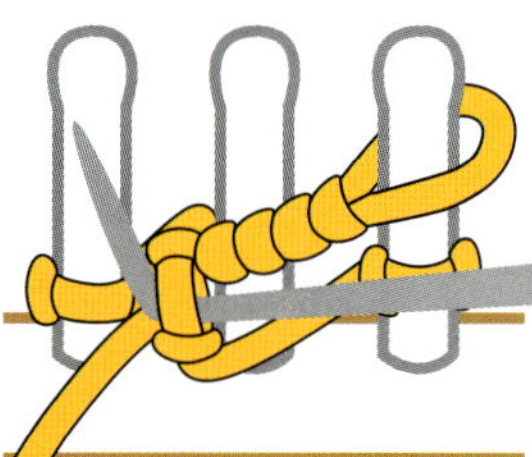

6 Move the stitch to the peg on the left. Then turn the loom so that the inside is facing you and, using your knitting tool, pick up the first stitch you hooked over and place it back on the peg. Then put the stitch you moved to the left peg back on peg 2.

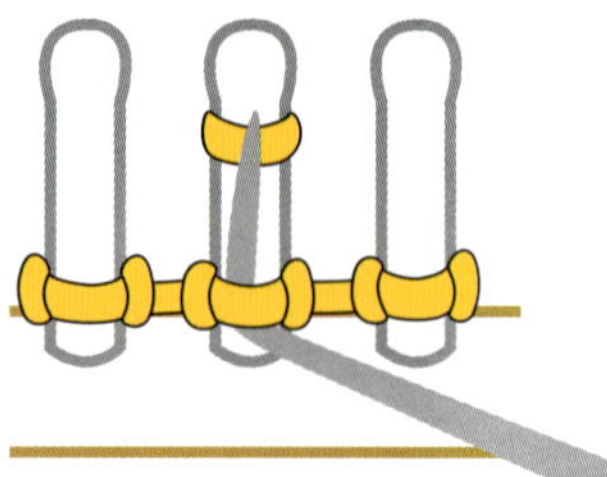

7 Turn the loom so you are working on the right side again, and hook the bottom stitch over the top to complete the bobble.

8 Repeat steps 2 to 7 around the loom so you have a bobble on every other peg. Knit 1 round.

9 On the next round, make a bobble on the first peg, k1. Repeat this sequence all the way around the loom. Knit 1 round.

10 Repeat the last 4 rounds 3 more times.

11 Knit 2 stitches together, k1, then repeat this sequence all around the loom so there are 14 stitches on the loom. Knit 1 round. Work a gather bind (cast) off (see page 10).

12 Stuff the pineapple and sew up the top using the cast-on yarn.

13 Cut a leaf-shaped edge along the felt strip, and then it roll up and secure with a few stitches.

14 Sew the leaf roll to the top of the pineapple, and then attach it to the key ring/bag charm.

TIP

To stop the stuffing coming through the holes in the knitting, use the toe of a pair of pantyhose, or some net to make a little bag, and place that in the pineapple before stuffing.

CHAPTER TWO

Bags and Cases

Watermelon cellphone cozy

A bright and colorful fruity cozy to keep your cellphone safe in your purse or protect it from accidental drops! With added sequins for a bit of sparkle.

YOU WILL NEED

- Sirdar Snuggly DK, 55% nylon/45% acrylic, light worsted (DK) yarn, 1¾oz (50g) balls, approx. 179yds (165m) per ball: 1 ball in each of Spicy Pink 350 (A), Playtime 532 (B), and Cream 303 (D)
- Sirdar Snuggly Replay DK, 50% cotton/50% acrylic, light worsted (DK) yarn, 1¾oz (50g) balls, approx. 164yds (150m) per ball: 1 ball of Hide-Out Green 130 (C)
- Sock loom, any size, with pegs set ¼in (6mm) apart
- US size E/4 (3.5mm) crochet hook
- Knitting tool
- Scissors
- Tapestry needle
- Black sequins
- Sewing needle and black thread
- Lime green button, ⅜in (1cm) diameter

SIZE

- Approx. 6in (15cm) long

INSTRUCTIONS

1 Cast on 23 stitches on one of the long sides of the sock loom using 2 strands of Playtime (B) and the cable cast on technique (see page 8).

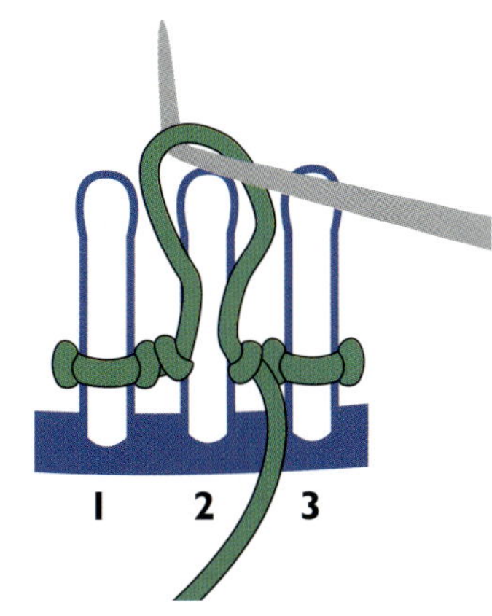

2 Knit stitch 1, then lift stitch 2 off the peg.

3 Place stitch 3 onto peg 2. Lift stitch 2 off the peg.

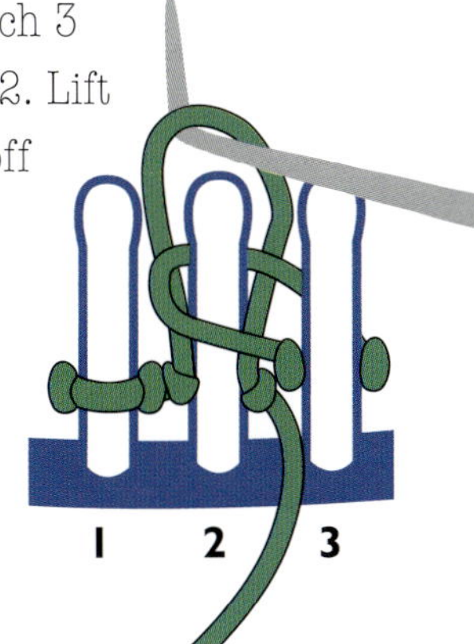

4 Place stitch 2 onto peg 3.

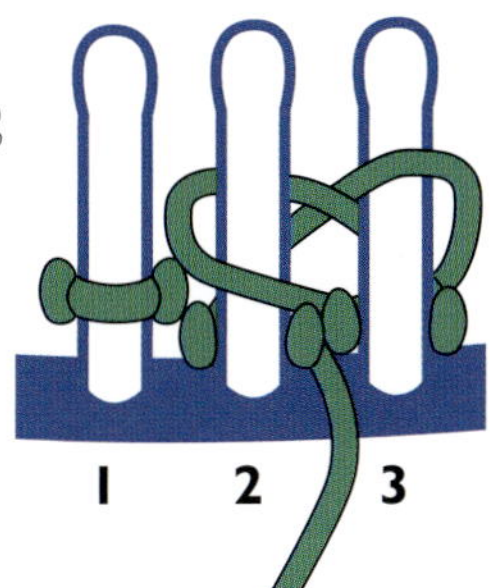

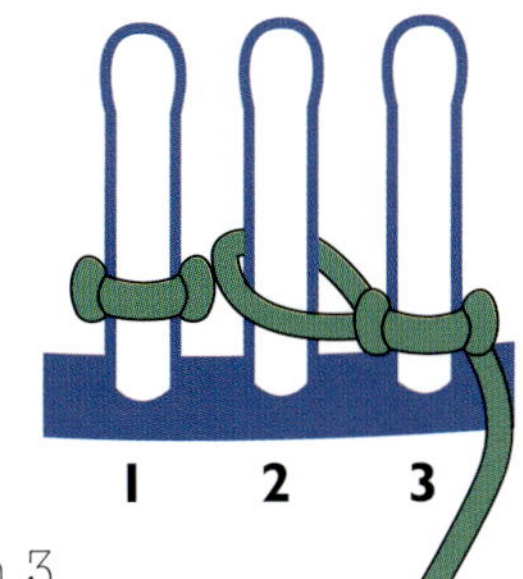

5 Knit stitch 3.

6 Repeat steps 2 to 5 (omitting the first knit stitch of the row) all along the row.

7 Repeat for 3 rows in Playtime (B).

8 Change one of the strands to Hide-Out Green (C) and work 2 rows.
Change the remaining Playtime (B) strand to Hide-Out Green (C) and work 2 rows.
Change one strand to Cream (D) and work 2 rows.
Change the remaining Hide-Out Green (C) strand to Cream (D) and work 2 rows.
Change both strands to Spicy Pink (A) and work 50 rows.

9 Repeat steps 8 to 7 in reverse order to make the other side of the watermelon skin.

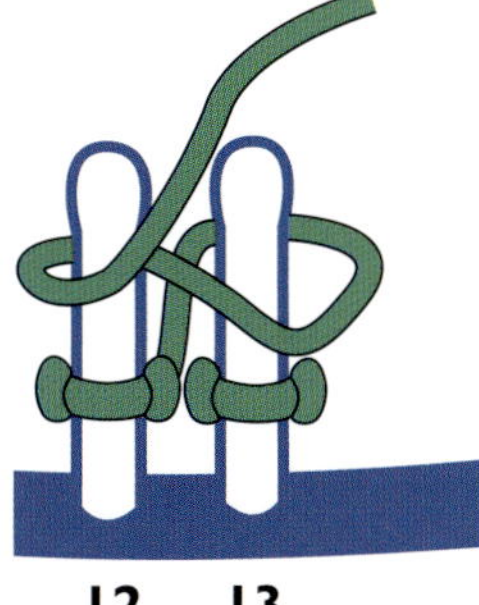

10 Bind (cast) off to stitch 11, then on stitches 12 and 13 work a figure-eight stitch (see page 13) for ¾in (2cm) on those 2 stitches for the button loop.

11 Bind (cast) off at the end of the loop, leaving a long end to sew it down later. Attach the Playtime (B) back onto stitch 14 using a slip knot, and bind (cast) off the rest of the row.

12 Using the black thread, sew the sequins to the pink section of the knitting, spacing them out to look like watermelon seeds.

13 Fold the piece of knitting in half, and sew up the sides.

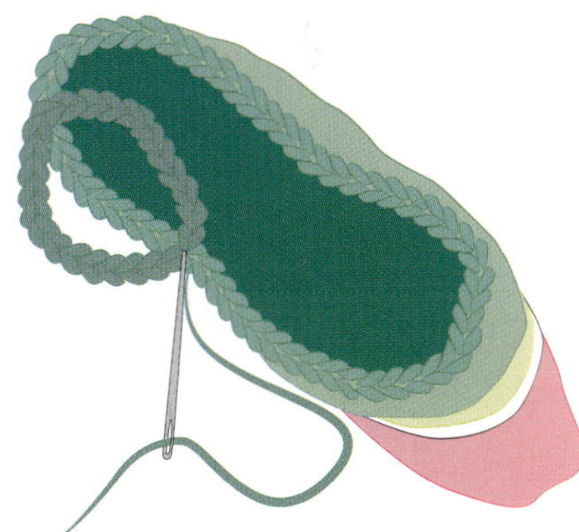

14 Turn the case inside out, and use the yarn end to attach the free end of the loop with a few stitches.

15 Turn right side out again. Sew the button to the opposite side of the case, to match the loop.

Pompom rucksack

This fun pompom-embellished rucksack is practical as well as quirky! Adjustable straps made from vintage fabric complete the look.

YOU WILL NEED

- DMC Natura XL, 100% cotton, super bulky (super chunky) yarn, 3½oz (100g) balls, approx. 82yds (75m) per ball: 3 balls of shade 109 (peach)
- Yarns and Colors Epic, 100% cotton, worsted (Aran) yarn, 1¾oz (50g) balls, approx. 82yds (75m) per ball: 1 ball in each of Orchid 052, Lollipop 036, and Pesto 085
- 10¼in (26cm) diameter round loom, with 82 pegs set ⅜in (9mm) apart
- Knitting tool
- Scissors
- 2 cardstock rings, 3¼in (8cm) diameter with central hole, or 3¼in (8cm) pompom maker
- Vintage fabric strips: four 60in (1.5m) x 1½in (4cm), and two 14in (35cm) x 1½in (4cm)
- 2 adjustable strap sliders, 1¼in (3cm) size
- 2 D-rings, 1¼in (3cm) size
- Sewing needle and white thread

SIZE

- Approx. 12in (30cm) wide x 15in (38cm) long

INSTRUCTIONS

1 Cast on 13 stitches using peach and the e-wrap technique (see page 9). Knit 1 row, purl 1 row.

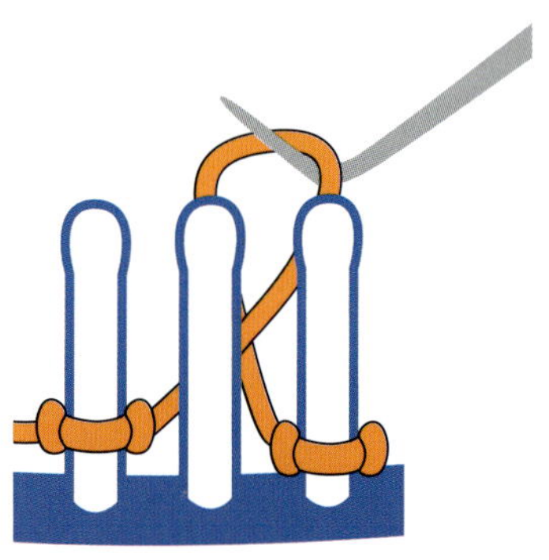

2 Increase twice on the next row, so move the first stitch on the loom onto the peg to the left, pick up the bar of the stitch on the row below, twist, and place on the empty peg. Move the last stitch onto the peg to the right, pick up the bar of the stitch on the row below, twist, and place on the empty peg. There are now 15 stitches on your loom. Knit 1 row, purl 1 row.

3 Repeat step 2 four more times so there are 23 stitches on your loom.

4 Work garter stitch (knit 1 row, purl 1 row) for 31 rows. This creates the flap of the bag. Using the e-wrap method, cast on the rest of the stitches and work garter stitch for 80 rows. This forms the body of the bag.

5 Knit 73 of the stitches on the round. You will be working on stitches 33 to 74 for the next section of the bag, the base. This will be worked in the same way that you make a toe for a sock.

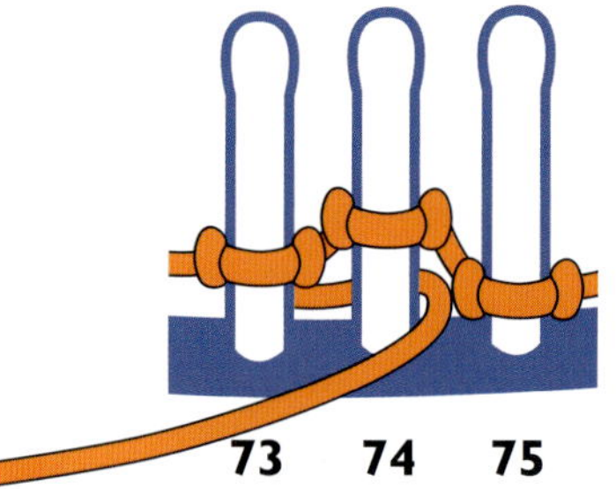

6 Lift stitch 74, wrap the yarn around the back of the peg, and replace the stitch.

7 Now purl back to stitch 32, lift stitch 33, and wrap the yarn around the back of the peg, then replace the stitch.

8 Repeat steps 5 to 7, knitting or purling one stitch less each time so that stitches 33 to 45 and stitches 74 to 62 all have 2 stitches on them, and the 15 stitches between only have one stitch.

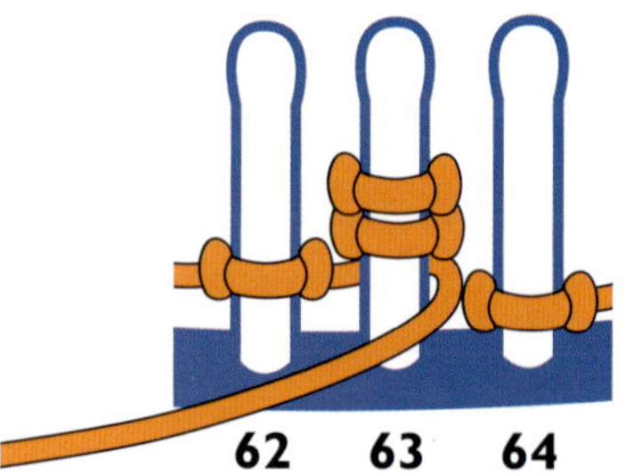

9 On the next row, knit to stitch 61, knit the 2 stitches on peg 62 as one, then lift the 2 stitches on peg 63, wrap the yarn around the back of the peg, and replace the 2 stitches so there are now 3 stitches on the peg.

10 Now purl back to peg 44, knit the 2 stitches on peg 45 as one, then lift the 2 stitches off peg 46, wrap the yarn around the back of the peg, and replace the 2 stitches, so you now have 3 stitches on the peg.

11 Repeat steps 9 and 10, knitting or purling one stitch more each time so that all the stitches eventually only have one stitch on them. This will form a cupped shape. Bind (cast) off.

12 Now make 2 pompoms (see page 17) using Orchid, 2 in Pesto, and 2 in Lollipop. Sew around the edge of the bag flap, using the lengths of peach yarn.

13 Cut 3 pieces of peach yarn each 1yd (1m) long and tie a knot 2in (5cm) from the end. Braid (plait) the entire length, and tie a knot 2in (5cm) from the other end. Fray the ends. Sew the braided cord around the top of the bag to create a drawstring closure.

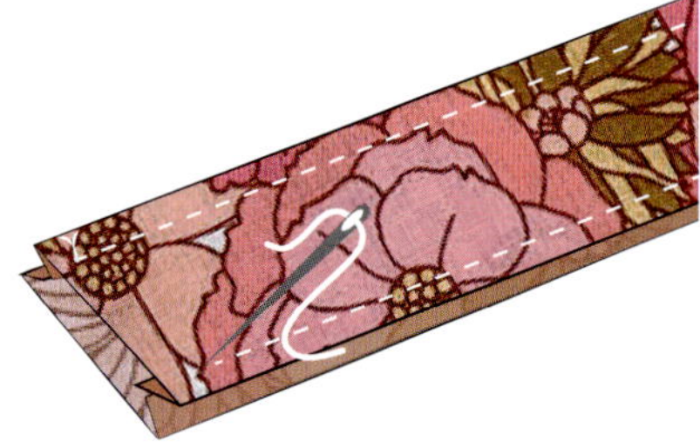

14 To make the straps, place two 60in (1.5m) x 1½in (4cm) pieces of fabric right sides together and sew the long sides ¼in (6mm) from the edge by hand or using a sewing machine. Turn right side out, press, and then topstitch along both edges of the strap, ⅛in (3mm) in from the edge. Repeat with the other two long pieces to make a second strap, then with the two 14in (35cm) pieces for the handle.

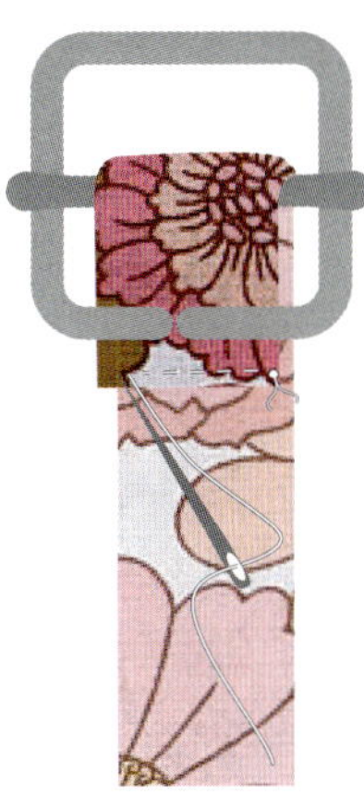

15 Thread the end of one of the straps over the center bar of an adjustable slider and sew in place. Repeat with a second strap and slider.

16 Thread a D-ring onto each end of the handle, fold over, and sew in place. Then thread the free end of a strap through one of the D-rings and then through the adjustable slider. Repeat with the other strap on the other end of the handle.

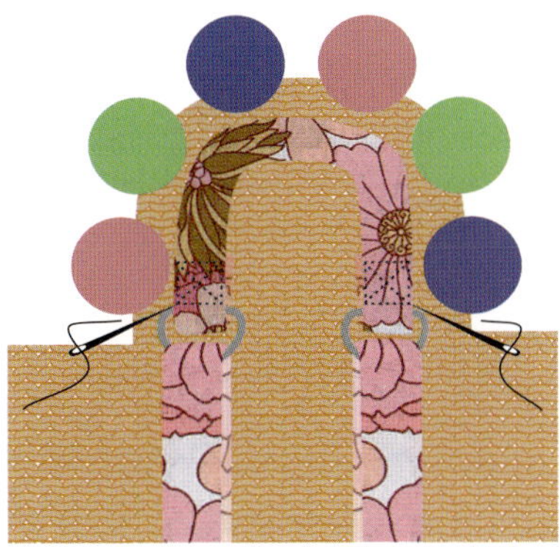

17 Sew the handle ends to the top of the bag just where the flap begins, using a box stitch and sewing just below the D-rings. Conceal the raw end of the handle under the box stitch.

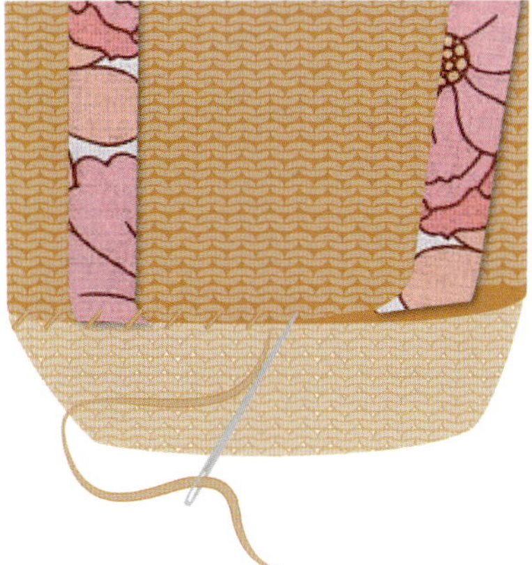

18 Insert the bottom end of each long strap into the opening at the bottom of the bag, one on each side, then sew the seam with slip stitch securing the handles at the same time.

Suede and silk purse

This cute little purse is knitted using linen stitch, a simple stitch that gives a woven fabric type effect. The purse is completed with a suede flap and mini tassel detail.

YOU WILL NEED

- Malabrigo Silky Merino, 50% silk/50% wool, light worsted (DK) yarn, 1¾oz (50g) balls, approx. 149yds (137m) per ball: 1 ball of Archangel 850
- 7¼ x 2in (18 x 5cm) sock loom, with 60 pegs set ¼in (6mm) apart
- US size E/4 (3.5mm) crochet hook
- Knitting tool
- Scissors
- Tapestry needle
- 12 x 6in (30 x 15cm) of patterned cotton fabric
- Sewing needle and white thread
- 6¼ x 4¾in (16 x 12cm) of light brown suede
- Leather needle and strong thread
- 1½in (4cm) square of gold leather
- Gold tassel cap
- Glue gun

SIZE

- Approx. 5½in (14cm) high x 5½in (14cm) wide

INSTRUCTIONS

1 Cast on 60 stitches, using the cable cast on technique (see page 8). Knit one round.

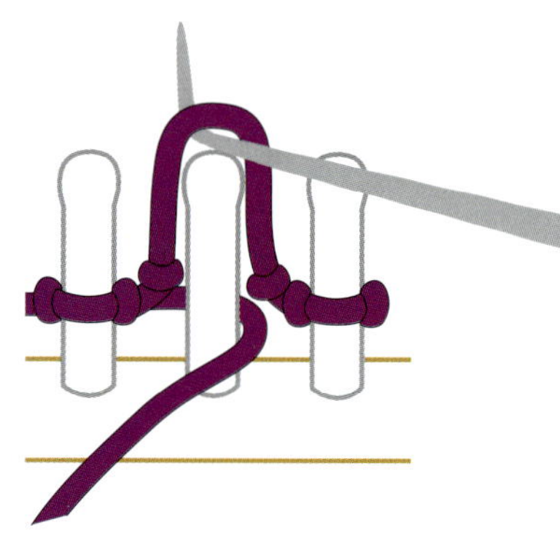

2 For round 2, work linen stitch as follows: knit 1 stitch, lift the next stitch off the peg, and wrap the working yarn behind the stitch.

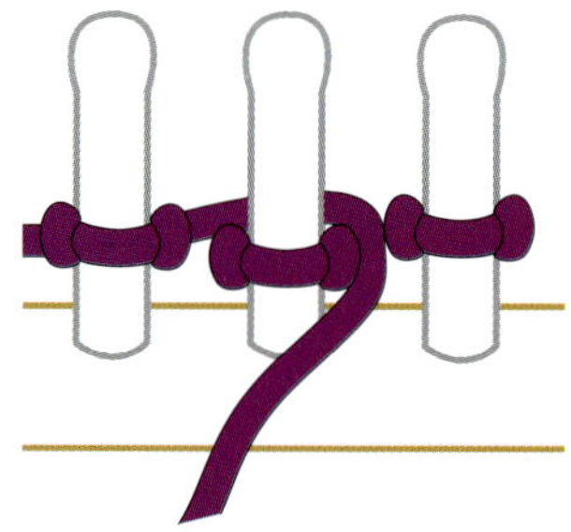

3 Place the stitch back onto the peg.

4 Repeat steps 2 and 3 for the whole round.

5 **For round 3**, knit.
For round 4, lift the stitch, wrap the yarn around the back of the peg, knit 1. Repeat all the way round.
For round 5, knit

6 Repeat these 4 rows (steps 2 to 5) until the piece is 6in (15cm) long.

7 Place half the stitches onto waste yarn, take them over and place them onto the opposite peg (so place stitch 1 on peg 60, stitch 2 on peg 59, and so on), until there are 2 stitches on pegs 60 to 31. Knit the bottom stitch over the top one to secure, and close the bottom of the bag. Bind (cast) off.

8 Using a length of yarn, sew up the two side seams of the bag.

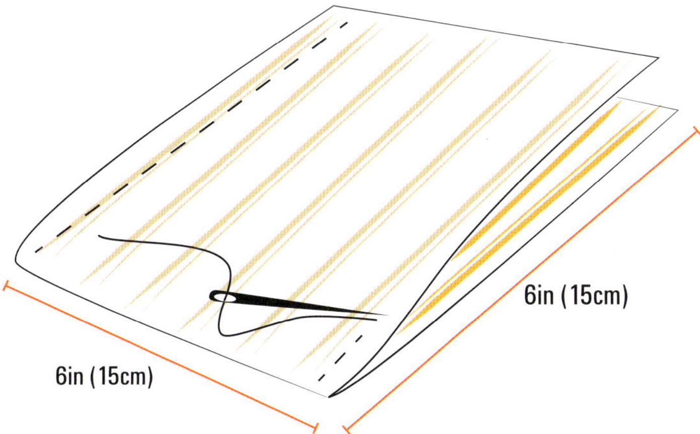

9 Fold the piece of fabric in half, right sides together, and sew along the sides to make a fabric lining, taking a $\frac{1}{4}$in (6mm) seam allowance. Fold over the top edge to the wrong side and press. Use the template on page 125 to cut a flap from the suede.

10 Place the fabric lining into the knitted piece with wrong sides together, and then insert the suede flap between the two layers. Sew the three layers together using the leather needle and sewing thread. Sew the other side of the lining to the knitting around the rest of the opening, using a normal needle and white thread.

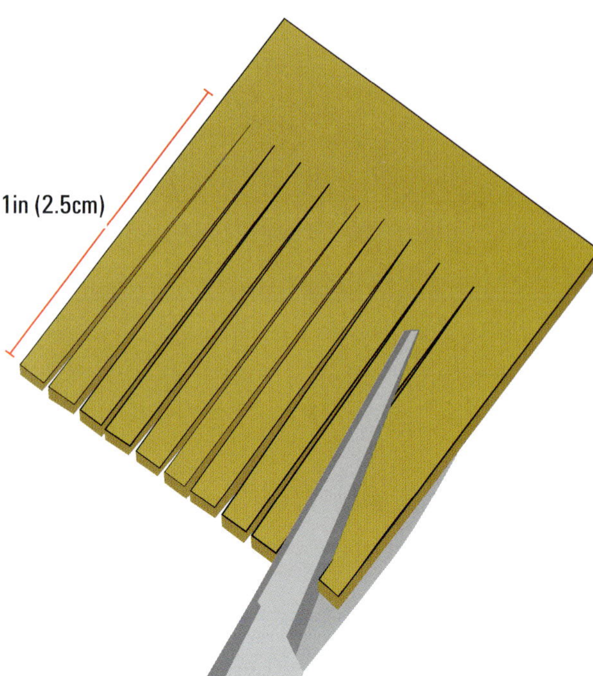

11 Cut 1in (2.5cm) long slits, each about ¼in (6mm) apart, in the small square of leather, being careful not to cut right through to the top.

12 Roll the leather piece up tightly and stick into the tassel cap using the glue gun.

13 Sew the tassel to the front of the flap using the leather needle.

Cable hot water bottle cover

Snuggle up on chilly evenings with this soft and cozy hot water bottle cover. With a cable knit design to challenge your loom knitting skills, it's not as hard as it looks—promise!

YOU WILL NEED

- Cascade Yarns 220 Superwash, 100% wool, light worsted (DK) yarn, 3½oz (100g) balls, approx. 220yds (200m) per ball: 2 balls of Lavender 1949
- 8½in (22cm) diameter round loom, with 72 pegs set ⅜in (9mm) apart
- Knitting tool
- Stitch holder
- Scissors
- Tapestry needle
- Hot water bottle
- 32in (80cm) of pink velvet ribbon, ⅜in (1cm) wide

SIZE

- 16½in (41cm) long x 7½in (19cm) wide (unstretched)

INSTRUCTIONS

1 Cast on 72 stitches using the e-wrap technique (see page 9).

2 Purl for 2 rounds.

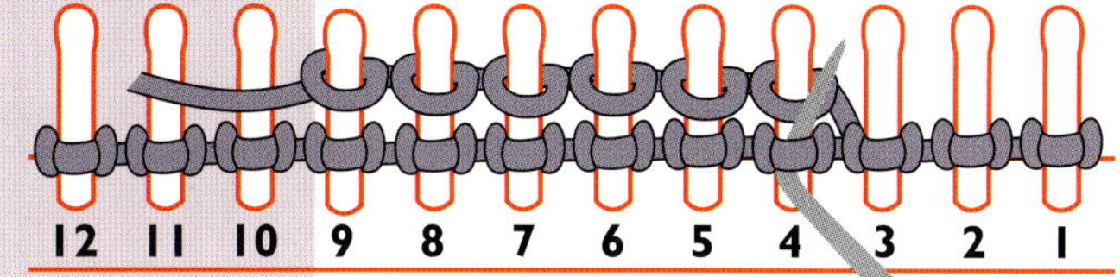

3 For round 1, purl 3, e-wrap knit 6 stitches, purl 3. Repeat this sequence around the loom 5 more times.

4 For round 2, purl 3, wrap the yarn twice around pegs 4 and 5, and knit the bottom stitch over the top 2 wraps, e-wrap knit stitches 6 to 9, purl 3. Repeat this sequence around the loom 5 more times.

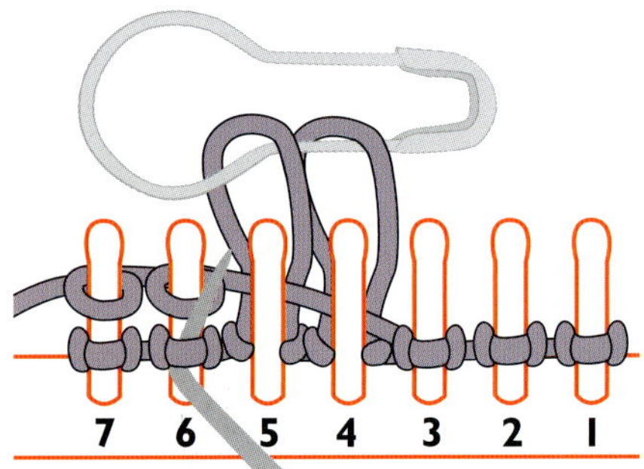

5 For round 3, purl 3, remove stitches 5 and 4 from the pegs (they are longer due to the double wrapping on the previous row), and place on the stitch holder, place the working yarn in front of stitches 4 and 5, e-wrap stitches 6 and 7.

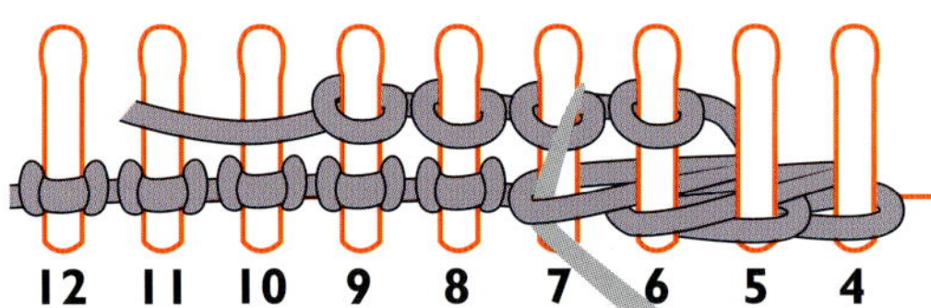

6 Place stitch 6 on peg 4 and stitch 7 on peg 5. Place stitch 4 on peg 6 and stitch 5 on peg 7. E-wrap stitches 6 to 9, purl 3. Repeat the sequence in steps 5 and 6 five more times around the loom.

7 For round 4, repeat round 1.

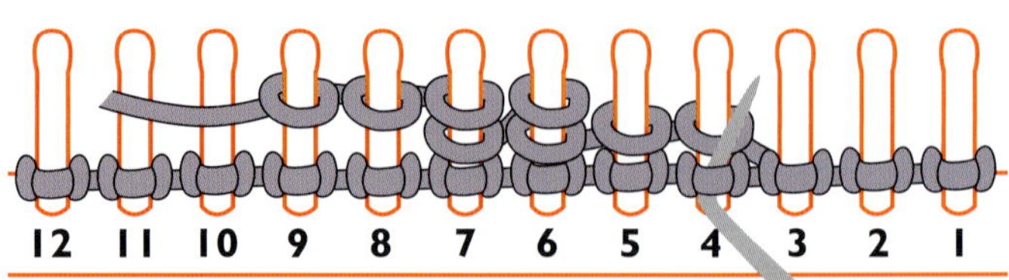

8 For round 5, purl 3, e-wrap knit pegs 4 and 5, double wrap pegs 6 and 7, and knit the bottom stitch over the top one on both pegs, e-wrap knit pegs 8 and 9, purl 3. Repeat the sequence 5 more times around the loom.

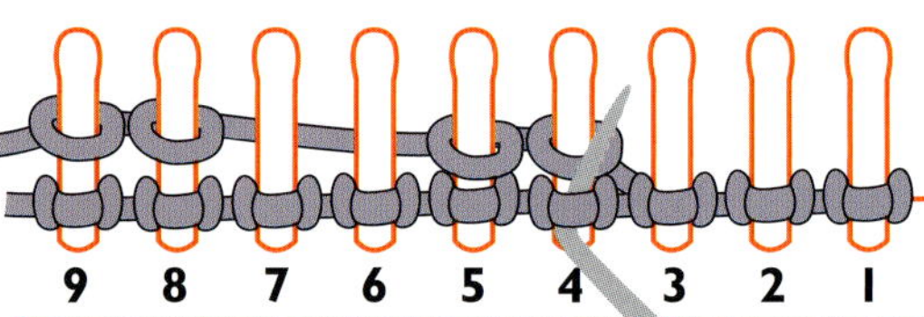

9 For round 6, purl 3, e-wrap knit stitches 4 and 5, skip pegs 6 and 7, e-wrap knit stitches 8 and 9.

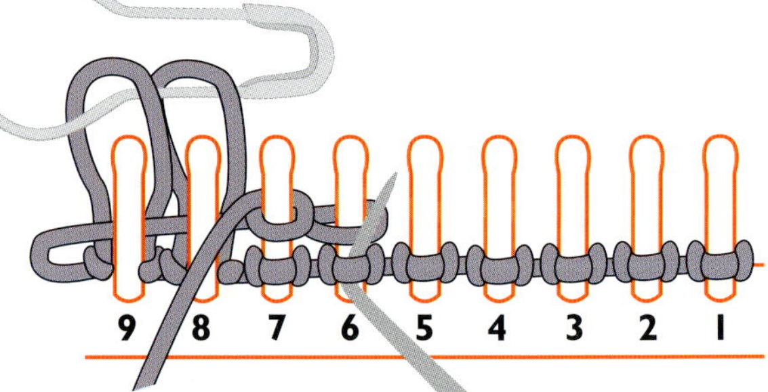

10 Place stitches 9 and 8 on the stitch holder. Bring the yarn to the front and e-wrap knit stitches 6 and 7.

11 Place stitch 7 on peg 9, stitch 6 on peg 8, stitch 8 on peg 6, and stitch 9 on peg 7, purl 3.

12 Repeat the sequence in steps 9 to 11 five more times around the loom.

13 Repeat rounds 1 to 6 (steps 3 to 12) 3 more times.

14 To create the extra ridge for the main part of the bottle cozy, on all rows e-wrap knit stitches 1 and 12 of each sequence. Then repeat rounds 1 to 6 for another 72 rounds.

15 On the next round, place stitches 1 to 36 on a piece of waste yarn and place them on the opposing pegs. So place stitch 1 onto peg 72, stitch 2 on peg 71, and so on. Knit the bottom stitch over the top one.

16 Bind (cast) off.

17 Thread the ribbon through holes in the knitting where the ridge begins. Pop your hot water bottle inside, pull the ribbon tight, and secure in place.

Knitted shopping bag

An open knit shopping bag, ideal for groceries. The faux leather handle gives it a slightly more sturdy and professional finish. It's worked using two strands of yarn held together for a firmer knit.

YOU WILL NEED

- Yarn and Colors Charming, 68% cotton/32% acrylic, fingering (4ply) yarn, 1¾oz (50g) balls, approx. 111yds (102m) per ball: 2 balls of Mustard 015
- Scrap of neon pink yarn
- 10¼in (26cm) diameter round loom, with 82 pegs set ⅜in (9mm) apart
- US size E/4 (3.5mm) crochet hook
- Knitting tool
- Scissors
- Tapestry needle
- 23in (58cm) orange faux leather bag handle

SIZE

- 10¾in (27cm) long x 11in (28cm) wide (unstretched)

INSTRUCTIONS

1 Using the ends of both balls of yarn held together, cast on 82 stitches using the cable cast on technique (see page 8). Work garter stitch (knit 1 row, purl 1 row) for 7 rows.

2 Begin using just one strand of yarn for the rest of the bag. Work a figure-eight stitch (see page 13) on pegs 2 and 1 by taking the yarn around the back of peg 2, bringing it around in front, and then around the back of peg 1, and then around the front of peg 1.

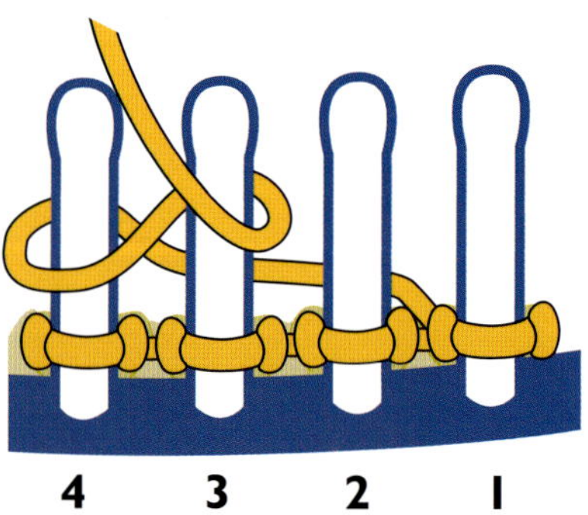

3 Repeat step 2, but on pegs 4 and 3. Repeat steps 2 and 3 around the loom.

4 Knit the next round.

5 K1, work figure-eight stitches around the loom, so you will be working on pegs 2 and 3, then 4 and 5, and so on around the loom, then knit the last stitch.
Knit the next round.

6 Repeat the 4 rounds (steps 2 to 5) until the bag measures approximately 10in (25cm), or to the desired size.

7 Repeat knit 2 stitches together, skip 1 stitch around the loom so there are 55 stitches left on the loom.

8 Repeat the pattern one more time—so repeat steps 2 to 5 for 4 rounds.

9 Gather bind (cast) off (see page 10).

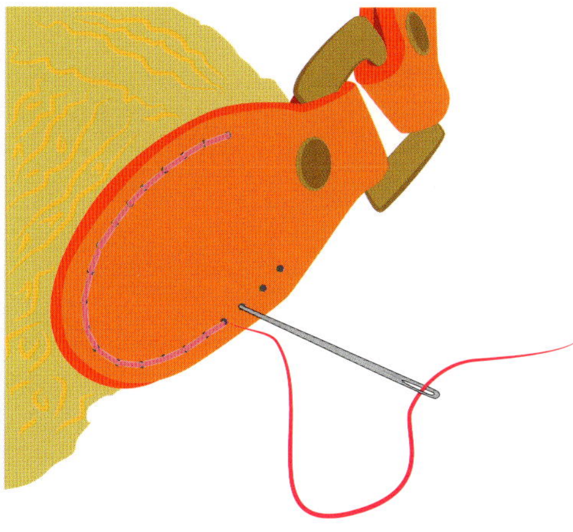

10 Using the neon pink yarn, sew the handle ends on either side of the bag to complete.

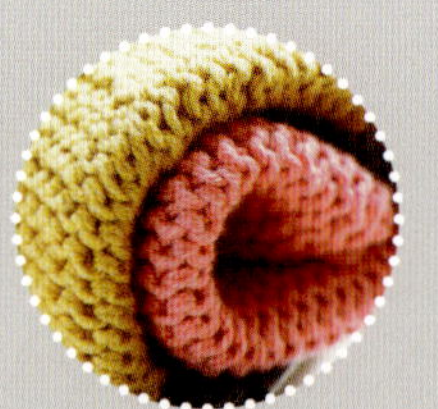

Geometric tablet cover

Protect your tablet from everyday bumps and bangs, with a soft, geometric, knitted cover. Worked using two strands of yarn held together for a cozy, thick knit.

YOU WILL NEED

- Drops Cotton Merino, 50% wool/50% cotton light worsted (DK) yarn, 1¾oz (50g) balls, approx. 120yds (110m) per ball: 1 ball of Mustard Yellow 15 (A), Water Pebbles 20 (B), and Raspberry Sorbet 36 (C)
- 6¼in (16cm) diameter round loom, with 52 pegs set ⅜in (9mm) apart
- Knitting tool
- Scissors
- Tapestry needle

SIZE

- 11in (28cm) long x 6½in (16cm) wide (unstretched)

INSTRUCTIONS

1 Wind half of one of the balls of yarn into a second ball. Then take a strand from each ball and wrap into a single ball of 2 strands. Repeat with all 3 colors.

2 Cast on 52 stitches, using 2 strands of mustard yarn (A) and the e-wrap cast on technique (see page 9).

3 Work garter stitch (knit 1 row, purl 1 row) for 20 rounds.

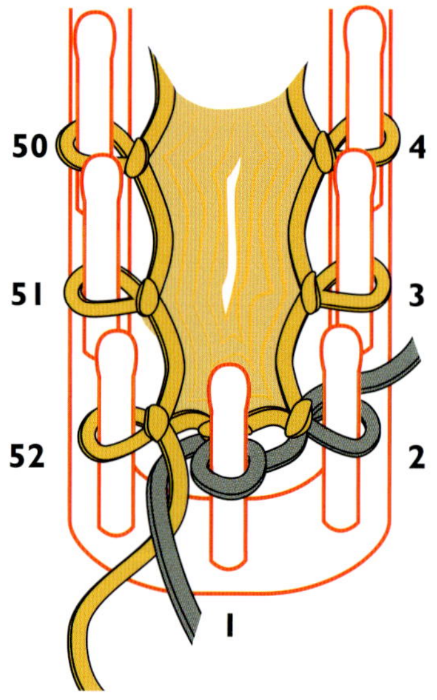

4 Add 2 strands of gray yarn (B), using a slip knot on peg 1, then knit stitches 1 and 2 in gray.

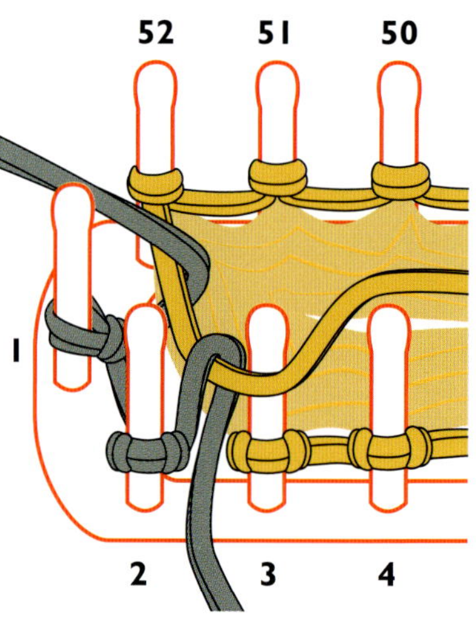

5 Twist the ends of the mustard and gray yarn, then knit 49 mustard stitches back to peg 51.

6 Purl back 3 gray stitches to peg 52. Twist the mustard and gray ends together and then purl using the mustard yarn back to peg 4.

7 Repeat the knit and purl rows backward and forward, adding one extra gray stitch on each round, until there are only gray stitches.

8 Knit 5 rows of garter stitch in gray.

9 Repeat steps 4 to 8, adding in the pink yarn (C).

10 Place stitches 1 to 26 onto a piece of waste yarn. Put stitch 1 onto peg 52, stitch 2 onto peg 51, and so on. Knit the bottom stitch over the top one. Bind (cast) off.

Japanese folded bag

Create a triangular-shaped folded bag, which is simple to both knit and construct. The ridged pattern on the knitted fabric emphasizes the cool construction technique.

YOU WILL NEED

- Lion Brand Hometown USA, 100% acrylic, super bulky (superchunky) yarn, 5oz (142g) balls, approx. 80yds (74m) per ball: 2 balls of Fort Worth Blue 109K
- 17in (43cm) long loom, with 48 pegs set ¾in (18mm) apart
- Knitting tool
- Scissors
- Tapestry needle
- 30 x 6in (75 x 15cm) of blue patterned fabric
- Sewing needle and blue thread
- Large bead

SIZE

- 12in (30cm) long x 12in (30cm) wide (unstretched)

INSTRUCTIONS

1 Cast on 32 stitches using the e-wrap technique (see page 9). For row 1, repeat k3, p1 to the end of the row. For row 2, repeat p1, k3 to the end of the row. Repeat these rows until you have a rectangle three times as long as it is wide. Bind (cast) off.

A E
D B C

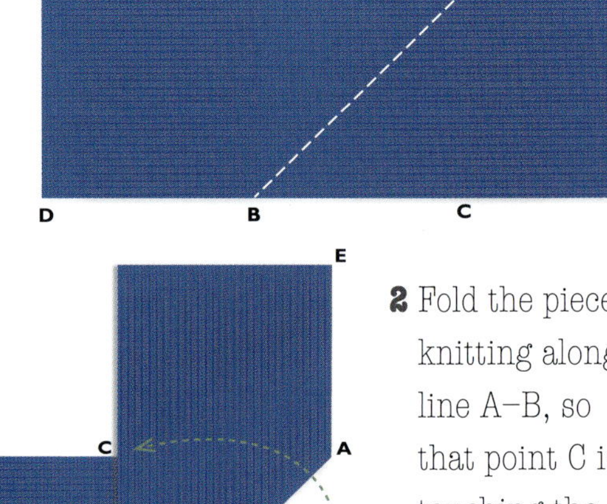

2 Fold the piece of knitting along line A–B, so that point C is touching the top edge.

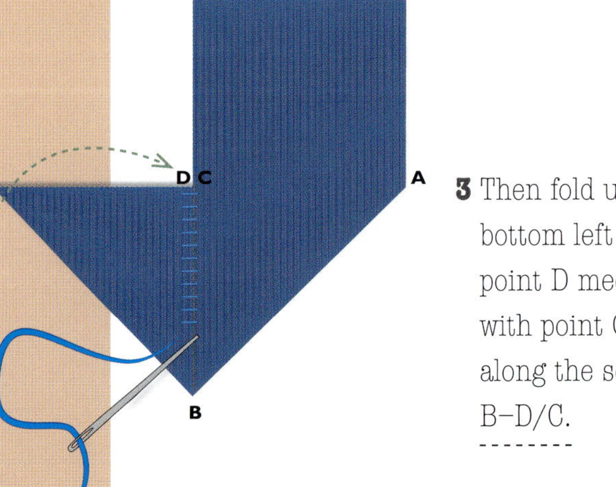

3 Then fold up the bottom left so that point D meets up with point C. Sew along the seam B–D/C.

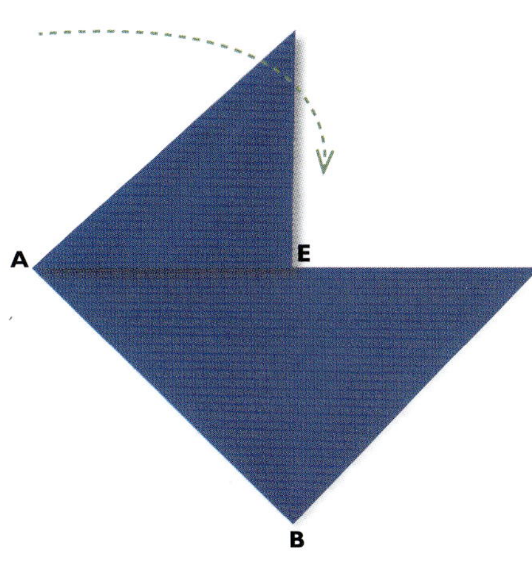

4 Turn the whole piece over and fold point E to the center. Sew along the seam.

5 Cut two template pieces (see page 124) from the fabric, and three 24 x 2in (60 x 5cm) strips.

6 To make the handle, fold one of the fabric strips in half with wrong sides together, and sew along the long side, ¼in (6mm) from the edge. Turn right side out to make a tube. Repeat with the other 2 strips and braid (plait) the 3 together.

7 Hem the top and the bottom of both trapezium pieces.

8 Fold each one in half with wrong sides together and sew the end seam. Turn right side out to make a fabric ring.

9 Thread one of the fabric rings onto one corner of the bag and insert one end of the braided handle. Sew all the layers together, securing the end of the handle at the same time. Repeat on the other corner of the bag with the second fabric ring and the other end of the handle.

10 To make the closure, sew a 4in (10cm) loop of thread at the join of D and C. Then turn the bag over and sew the large bead to the front of the bag in a matching position.

CHAPTER THREE

For Kids

Butterfly bunting

A cute length of butterfly bunting, ideal for a child's bedroom or playroom. It's made using a traditional "Knitting Nancy"—why not get your little ones to help?

YOU WILL NEED

- Stylecraft Special DK, 100% acrylic, light worsted (DK) yarn, 3½oz (100g) balls, approx. 322yds (295m) per ball:
  1 ball each of Aspen 1422, Matador 1010, Magenta 1084, Citron 1263, Shrimp 1132, Sage 1725, Spice 1711, and Petrol 1708
- 1in (2.5cm) diameter round loom, with 5 pegs set ¾in (18mm) apart
- 7yds (6.3m) of ¼in (6mm) cord, cut into 9 equal lengths
- Knitting tool
- Scissors
- Sewing needle and thread

SIZE

- Approx. 46in (118cm) long

INSTRUCTIONS

1 Cast on 5 stitches, using any color and the e-wrap technique (see page 9).

2 Knit for 2in (5cm), then insert one of the lengths of cord down into the tube you have made.

3 Continue knitting until the piece measures 24in (60cm), enclosing the cord as you go, then change to a contrast color and knit for another 4in (10cm).

4 Work a gather bind (cast) off (see page 10). Sew in all the loose ends, and close the first end, making sure the cord is completely concealed by the knitted tube. Make another eight pieces using different color combinations, using the photo as a guide.

5 Bend the first tube into the butterfly shape as shown, with the first color as the wings and the second color folded around and up to create the body and head. Sew in place using the sewing needle and thread, trying to make sure the stitches are as small and invisible as possible.

6 With the next piece, and each one afterward, thread the tube through the wing of the adjacent butterfly to link them before bending into the butterfly shape.

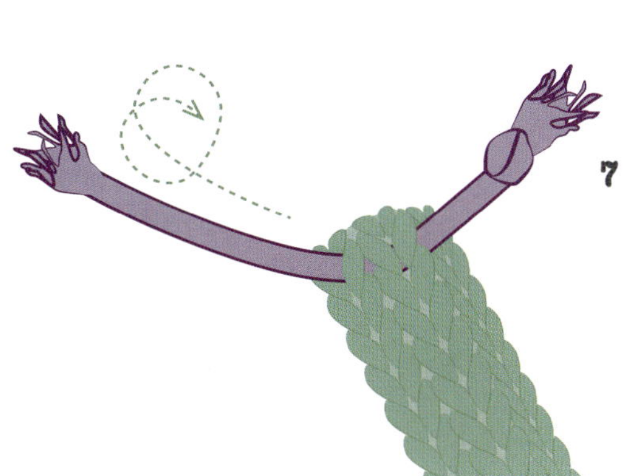

7 To make the antennae, thread a short length of contrasting yarn through the top of the body and knot each end. Trim to size.

Cat socks

These snuggly socks are the perfect lazy weekend accessory for older kids. The cute ears are knitted separately and attached to the loom during the knitting.

YOU WILL NEED

- Stylecraft Special DK, 100% acrylic, light worsted (DK) yarn, 3½oz (100g) balls, approx. 322yds (295m) per ball: 1 ball each of Aspen 1422 (A), Spice 1711 (B), and Parchment 1218 (C)
- Scrap of gray yarn for features
- 7¼ x 2in (18 x 5cm) sock loom, with 44 pegs set ¼in (6mm) apart
- Knitting tool
- Tapestry needle
- Scissors
- Pink felt
- Sewing needle and pink thread

SIZE

- To fit shoe sizes US 6–9 (UK 4–7)

INSTRUCTIONS

1 Wind half of one of the balls of yarn into a second ball. Then take a strand from each ball and wrap into a single ball of 2 strands. Repeat with all 3 colors. Using 2 strands of Aspen (A) held together, cast on 44 stitches using the e-wrap technique (see page 9).

2 Work in k2, p2 rib for 12 rounds.

3 For the next 40 rounds, work in knit only.

4 Now start to shape the heel using the short row shaping technique below. You will only be using the first 22 stitches on the loom.

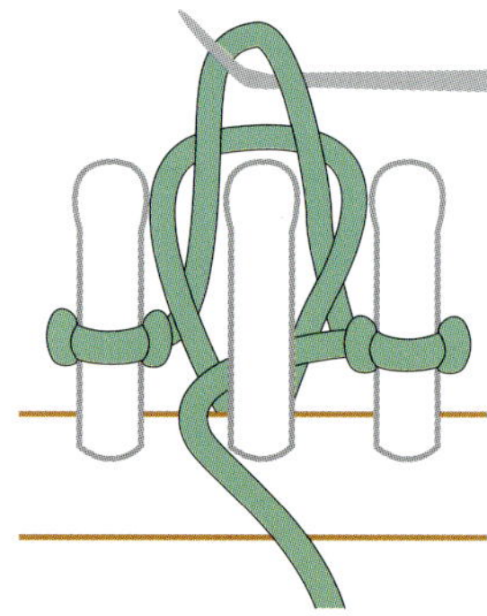

5 Knit stitches 1 to 21, then lift the 22nd stitch off the peg and wrap the yarn around the back of the peg.

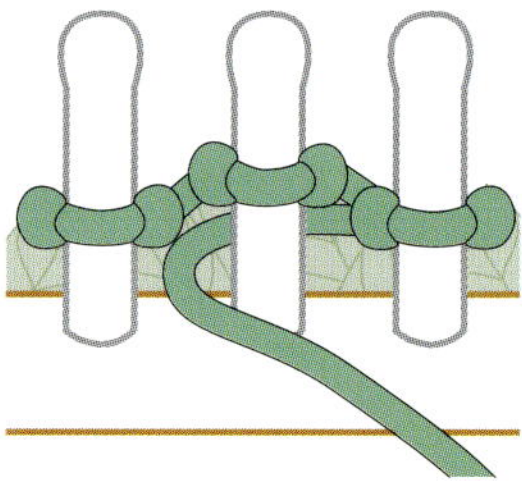

6 Replace the stitch on the peg so that the yarn ends are at the front of the work.

7 Now knit back from stitch 21 to stitch 2, then lift the first stitch, wrap the yarn, and replace the stitch again as in steps 5 and 6.

8 Repeat steps 5 to 7, knitting one less stitch on each row and wrapping the following stitch, until you have 7 wrapped stitches at the start and 7 wrapped stitches at the end of your row of 22 stitches, and 8 stitches left as singles in the middle.

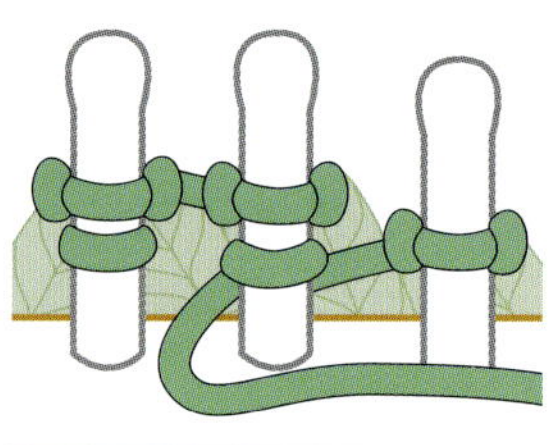

9 On the next row, knit stitches 8 to 15, then knit the 2 stitches on peg 16 as one stitch, lift the 2 stitches on peg 17, wrap the yarn around the back of the peg, and replace the 2 stitches so there are now 3 stitches on peg 17.

10 Knit stitches 15 to 8, then knit the 2 stitches on peg 7 as one stitch, lift the 2 stitches on peg 6, wrap and replace both stitches so there are now 3 stitches on peg 6.

11 Knit stitches 8 to 16, knit all 3 stitches on peg 17 as one, then lift the 2 stitches on peg 18, wrap, and replace the stitches. Knit stitches 17 to 7, then knit all 3 stitches on peg 6, lift the 2 stitches on peg 5, wrap and replace the stitches.

12 Keep repeating step 11, working one more stitch on each row, until all the pegs only have one stitch on them again and you are back at stitch 22. Your heel has been formed.

13 To reinforce the heel, lift stitch 23, wrap the yarn around the back of the peg as you did in steps 5 and 6, replace the stitch, and knit left to right back to stitch 1. Lift stitch 44 (the stitch to the right of stitch 1) and wrap the yarn around the back of the peg and replace the stitch.

14 Continuing to use Aspen (A), knit 10 rounds, treating the 2 stitches on pegs 23 and 44 as one stitch.

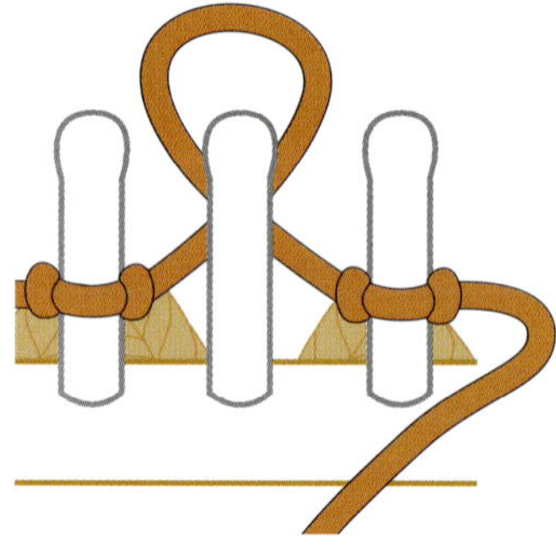

15 Now make the ears. On a separate part of the loom, cast on 2 stitches in Spice (B). Knit 3 rows. Increase once by moving the first stitch to the next peg on the right, pick up the horizontal bar of yarn between the 2 stitches, twist, and place on the empty peg so there are now 3 stitches.

16 Knit for 3 rows, then on the next row increase once more as in step 15 so there are 4 stitches. Knit for another 3 rows, then on the next row increase once more, so you have an ear that is 5 stitches wide. Make a second ear on another set of empty pegs.

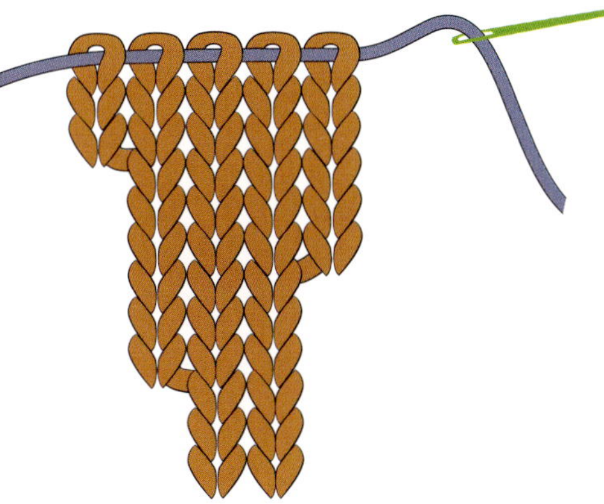

17 Take a piece of waste yarn, thread through the stitches of each ear, and remove from the loom.

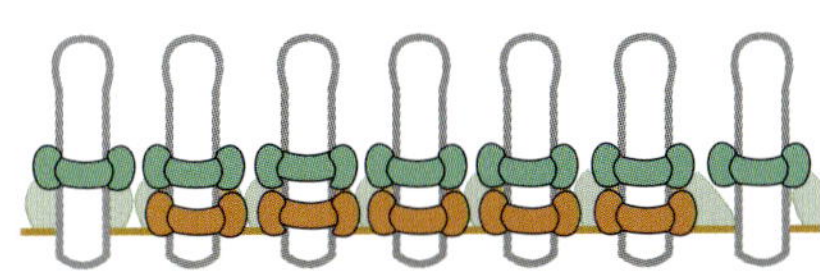

18 Remove the stitches from pegs 27 to 31 and place one set of ear stitches on those pegs, making sure they are right side up. Replace the original stitches. Do the same with the other ear on pegs 36 to 40.

19 Join in 2 strands of Spice (B), and with both strands held together knit for 28 rounds, treating the 2 stitches on the ear pegs as one stitch on the first round.

20 To create the chest, work the first 28 stitches of the round in Spice (B), then join 2 strands of Parchment (C) on peg 29, knit 8 stitches and then change back to Spice (B) for the rest of the round.

21 Over the next 14 rounds, gradually expand the size of the chest by one stitch per round, until stitches 23 to 44 are in Parchment (C).

22 Using Parchment (C), knit the toe as for the heel (steps 4 to 12), but working on stitches 23 to 44 so that the seam of the toe will be under the ball of the foot.

23 Knit 2 rounds with Parchment (C). Bind (cast) off.

24 Sew the toe seam to complete the sock.

25 Make French knot eyes (see page 16) in gray yarn. Sew long stitches in gray for whiskers, then take tiny stitches at intervals over each stitch to hold it down.

26 Cut a small nose shape from the pink felt and sew to the face using pink thread.

27 Repeat all the steps to make a second sock.

Knitted rag doll

This cute little dolly can be personalized to suit whoever you are making it for, by changing the hair color or skin tone. Add accessories, or change the dress pattern if you are feeling adventurous.

YOU WILL NEED

- Rico Essentials Cotton DK, 100% cotton, light worsted (DK) yarn, 1¾oz (50g) balls, approx. 131yds (120m) per ball: 1 ball each of Nude 052 (A), Berry 015 (B), and Turquoise 033 (D)
- Rico Creative Cotton DK, 100% cotton, light worsted (DK) yarn, 1¾oz (50g) balls, approx. 126yds (115m) per ball: 1 ball each of Pistachio 016 (C) and Orange 007 (E)
- Scraps of yellow, teal, and red yarn for bows and features
- Sock loom, any size, with pegs set ¼in (6mm) apart
- US size E/4 (3.5mm) crochet hook
- Knitting tool
- Scissors
- Tapestry needle
- Toy stuffing

SIZE

- Approx. 13½in (34cm) tall

INSTRUCTIONS

1 Start by making the legs. Set the sock loom to 16 pegs, and cast on 16 stitches, using Pistachio (C) and the e-wrap technique (see page 9).

2 Knit 5 rounds with Pistachio (C), then change to Turquoise (D) and knit 5 rounds. Repeat 4 more times.

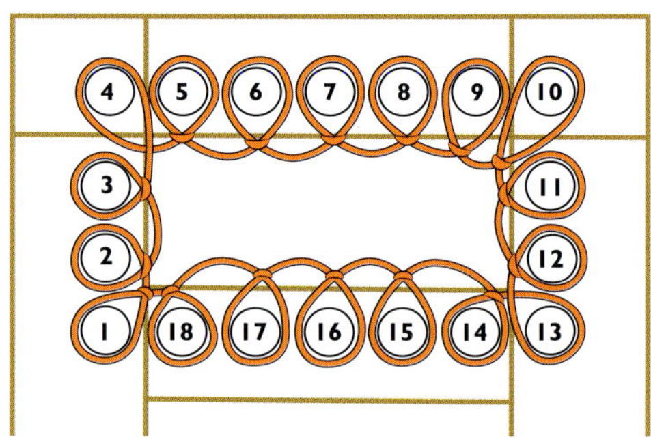

3 Change to Orange (E), increase the loom to 18 pegs, and cast on stitches to pegs 4 and 13. Knit 1 round.

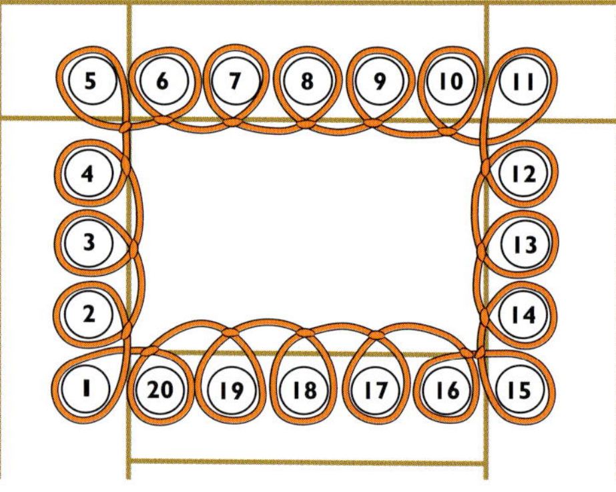

4 Increase the loom to 20 pegs and cast on stitches to pegs 1 and 11. Knit 1 round.

5 Knit 14 rounds.

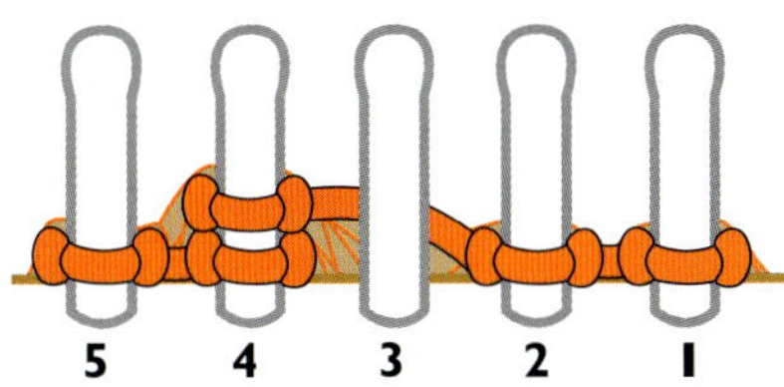

6 Decrease the foot by 5 stitches: skip 2 stitches, knit 2 stitches together by placing the next stitch onto the following peg, and repeat around the loom so there are 15 stitches in the round. Knit 1 round and then work a gather bind (cast) off (see page 10). Make a second leg.

7 To make the arms, cast on 16 stitches using Nude (A) and the e-wrap technique, and knit 40 rounds. Increase to make the hands as you did with the feet (steps 3 to 6), but working only in Nude (A). Make a second arm.

8 To make the body, set the loom to 28 pegs and cast on 28 stitches using Nude (A) and the e-wrap technique. Knit for 30 rounds.

9 To make holes to insert the arms, on the next 18 rows knit backward and forward in rows on stitches 1 to 14 rather than all the way around the loom. Cut the yarn.

10 Reattach the yarn on peg 15 and knit 19 rows, working between pegs 15 to 28 only, to make the back of the body. You should end up at peg 28.

11 You'll now shape the head. Decrease to 26 stitches by knitting 2 stitches together on pegs 9 and 23. Move all the stitches next to each other so there are no gaps. Knit 1 round across all stitches.

12 Decrease to 24 stitches by knitting 2 stitches together on pegs 1 and 14. Move all the stitches next to each other so there are no gaps. Knit 1 round.

13 Decrease to 18 stitches by knitting 2 stitches together on pegs 4, 8, 12, 16, 20, and 24. Move all the stitches next to each other so there are no gaps. Knit 4 rounds. Now increase to 20 stitches by moving the stitches so there are empty pegs between pegs 3 and 5 and pegs 12 and 14, then pick up the bar of the stitch on the row below and place on the empty peg so there are new stitches on pegs 4 and 13. Knit 1 round. Increase to 22 stitches by adding stitches on pegs 1 and 11 in the same way as before. Knit 1 round. Increase to 24 stitches by adding stitches on pegs 6 and 17. Knit for 20 rounds.

14 On the next 3 rounds decrease by 2 stitches on each round until there are 18 stitches again, by knitting 2 stitches together on opposite corners as you have been doing previously. Work a gather bind (cast) off.

15 Stuff the arms, insert them into the armholes, and stitch them in place.

16 Stuff the body and legs, then insert the legs into the bottom of the body and sew in place. Add a bow of yellow yarn to each shoe.

17 Sew a face onto the doll using teal and French knots (see page 16) for eyes, red and backstitch (see page 16) for the mouth, and Nude (A) for the nose, following the photo as a guide.

18 Cut 10in (25cm) lengths of Orange (E) for the hair. Fold a pair of strands in half and thread the loop into a tapestry needle. Pull the loop through one of the stitches on the head, then remove the needle and pull the strand ends through the loop to knot in place. Repeat all over the head.

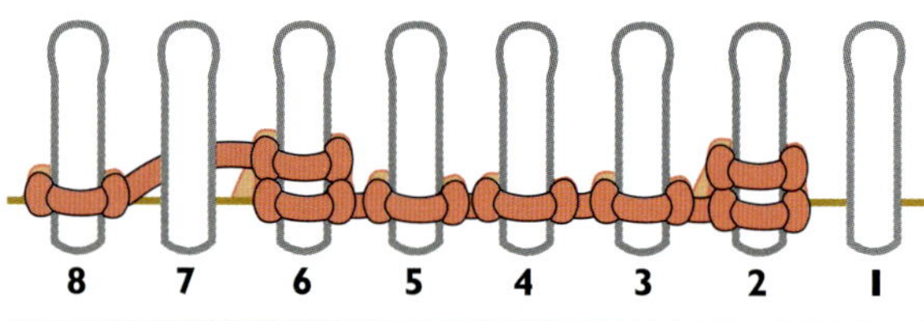

19 For the dress, cast on 40 stitches, using Berry (B) and the cable cast on method (see page 8).

Rounds 1 and 3: Repeat k1, p1 to the end.

Rounds 2 and 4: Repeat p1, k1 to the end.

Round 5: Lift stitch 2, place stitch 1 on peg 2 and replace stitch 2, knit stitches 3 to 5, place stitch 7 on stitch 6, knit stitch 8. E-wrap pegs 1 and 7 as you knit the round, and knit the 2 stitches on pegs 2 and 6 as one stitch. Repeat 4 more times around the loom.

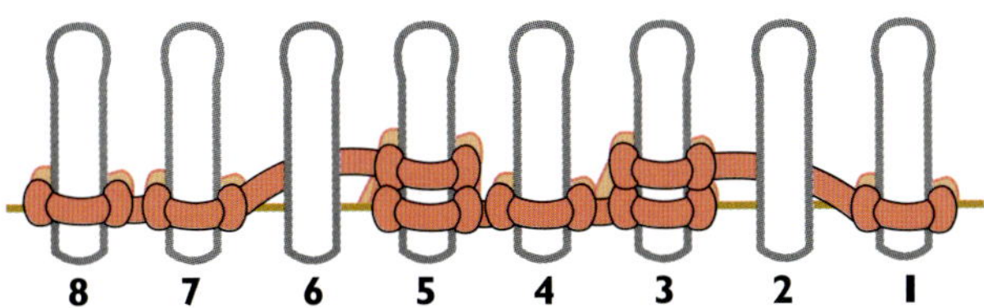

20 For **rounds 6, 8, 10, 16, 18, and 20**: Knit.
Round 7: Knit stitch 1, lift stitch 3, place stitch 2 on peg 3 and replace stitch 3, knit stitch 4, place stitch 6 on stitch 5, knit stitches 7 and 8. E-wrap pegs 2 and 6 as you knit the round and knit the 2 stitches on pegs 3 and 5 as one stitch. Repeat 4 more times around the loom.

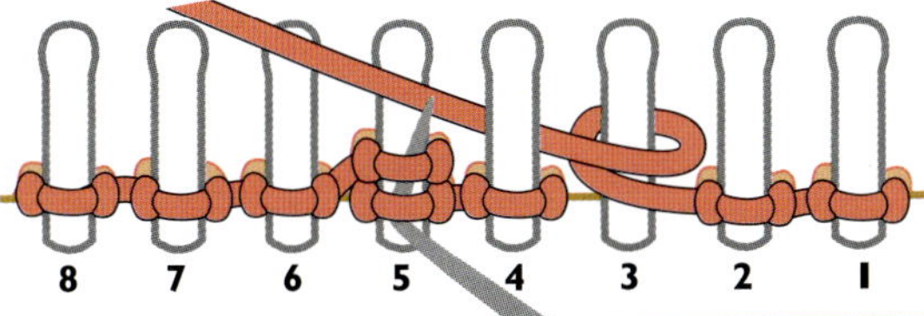

21 Round 9: Knit stitches 1 and 2, move stitch 4 onto peg 5, move stitch 3 onto peg 4, e-wrap peg 3, skip stitch 4, and knit the 2 stitches on peg 5 as one stitch.

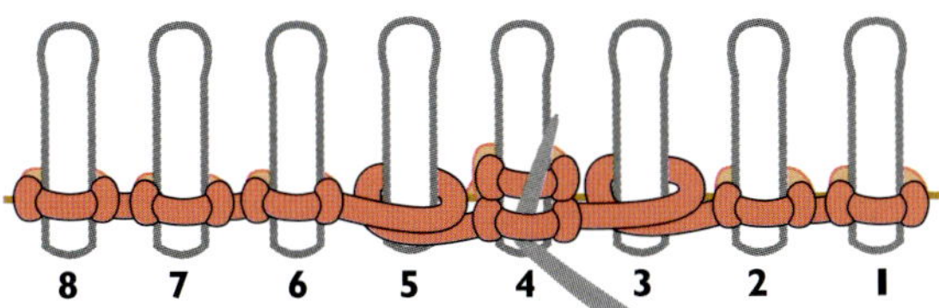

22 Then move the hooked stitch 5 onto peg 4, and hook the bottom stitch over the top one. E-wrap peg 5 and knit stitches 6 to 8. Repeat steps 20 and 21 four more times around the loom.

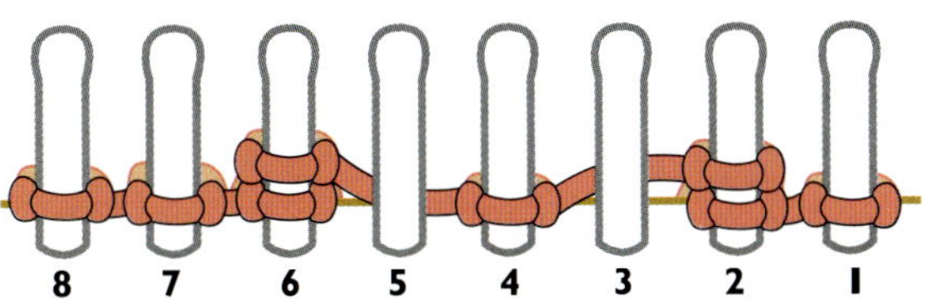

23 Rounds 11 and 13: K1, p1 to the end.
Rounds 12 and 14: P1, k1 to the end.
Round 15: Knit stitch 1, lift stitch 2, place stitch 3 on peg 2 and replace stitch 2, knit stitch 4, place stitch 5 on peg 6, knit stitches 7 and 8. E-wrap pegs 3 and 5 as you knit the round and work the 2 stitches on pegs 2 and 6 as one stitch. Repeat 4 more times around the loom.

24 Round 17: Lift stitch 1, place stitch 2 on peg 1 and replace stitch 1, knit stitches 3 to 5, lift stitch 7, place stitch 6 on peg 7 and replace stitch 7, knit stitch 8. E-wrap pegs 2 and 6 as you knit the round and work the 2 stitches on pegs 1 and 7 as one stitch. Repeat 4 more times around the loom.

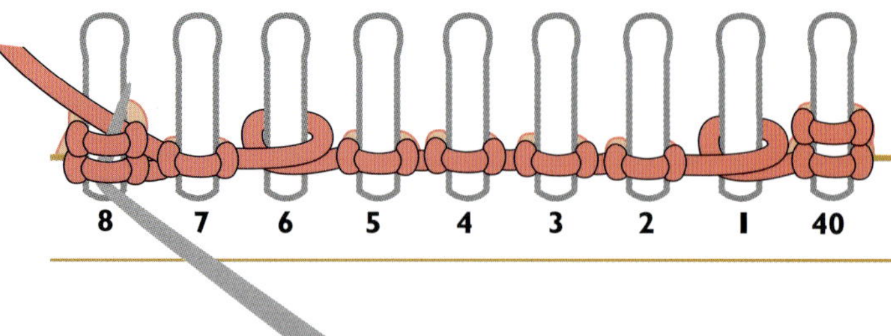

25 **Round 19**: Move stitch 1 backward to stitch 40, e-wrap peg 1, knit stitches 2 to 5, move stitch 7 onto peg 8, move stitch 6 onto peg 7, and e-wrap empty peg 6. Knit both stitches on peg 8 as one stitch. Repeat 4 more times around the loom.

26 Knit stitches 1 to 6. Move the stitch on peg 8 to peg 7 and knit the bottom stitch on peg 7 over the top one, e-wrap the empty peg 8. Repeat 4 more times around the loom.

Repeat rounds 1 to 20 again.

Repeat rounds 1 to 4 once more to complete the pattern on the skirt.

27 Decrease the number of stitches on the loom by knitting 2 stitches together, then knitting the next 2 stitches, and repeating this sequence around the whole loom. You'll have 30 stitches.

To create the armholes, knit backward and forward in rows on stitches 1 to 15 for 20 rows, then repeat on pegs 16 to 30. Knit 1 stitch, then decrease the number of stitches on the loom by knitting 2 stitches together, then knitting the next 2 stitches, and repeating this sequence around the whole loom to the last stitch, and knit 1. You'll have 23 stitches.

28 Change to Turquoise (D). Knit 1, then reduce number of stitches on the loom by knitting 2 stitches together, then knitting the next 2 stitches, and repeating this sequence around the whole loom to the last 2 stitches, knit the last 2 stitches together. You'll have 17 stitches. Now begin working in rounds to create the collar, so knit for 4 rounds. Bind (cast) off. Place the dress on the doll to complete.

Mary Jane slippers

Keep teen feet snug and warm in these chunky knit Mary Jane-style slippers. The suede soles ensure they are hardwearing, and you won't be slipping all over the floor!

YOU WILL NEED

- Cascade Yarns Pacific Chunky, 60% acrylic/40% wool, bulky (chunky) yarn, 3½oz (100g) balls, approx. 120yds (110m) per ball:
  1 ball each of Dusty Turquoise 23 (A) and and Ruby 43 (B)
- 4¾in (12cm) diameter round loom, with 44 pegs set ⅜in (9mm) apart
- Knitting tool
- Scissors
- 2 covered buttons, ⅝in (15mm) diameter
- 2 circles of patterned fabric, 1in (25mm) diameter
- Sewing needle and white thread
- Pair of suede soles
- Pair of faux sheepskin inners
- Superglue/hot glue gun
- Tapestry needle

SIZE

- To fit shoe sizes US 5½–6½ (UK 4–5)

INSTRUCTIONS

1 To make a smaller or larger pair of slippers, reduce or increase the measurements by 1in (2.5cm). The slippers are fairly stretchy so exact measurements aren't required. Wind a separate small ball of Dusty Turquoise (A) to use for the toe later.

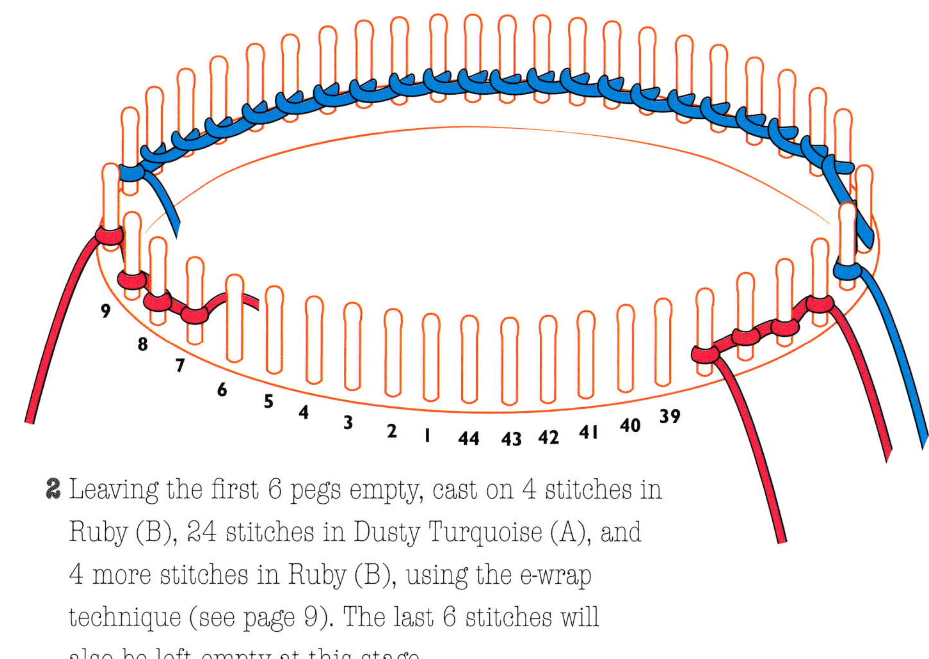

2 Leaving the first 6 pegs empty, cast on 4 stitches in Ruby (B), 24 stitches in Dusty Turquoise (A), and 4 more stitches in Ruby (B), using the e-wrap technique (see page 9). The last 6 stitches will also be left empty at this stage.

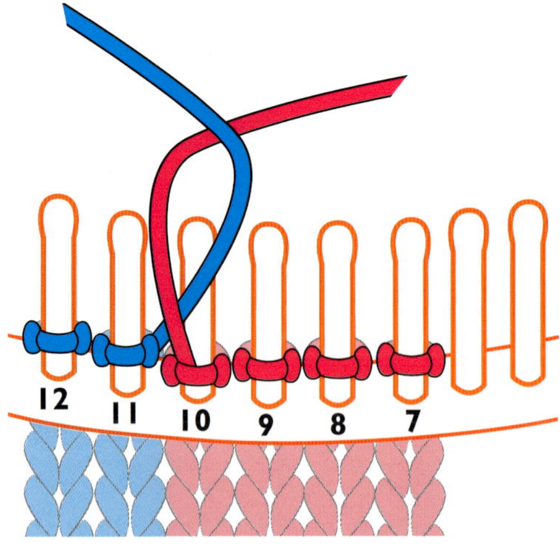

3 Using the e-wrap knitting technique, knit one row counterclockwise and then the next one clockwise for 4½in (12cm). Remember to twist the yarns together as you change color so there are no holes in the piece.

4 Cast on the 12 empty pegs using the e-wrap technique and Ruby (B). On the second slipper, cast on the strap from the other side so that the strap is on the opposite side when made up.

5 Changing colors as established, e-wrap knit (see page 12) to the other side of the slipper and back again.

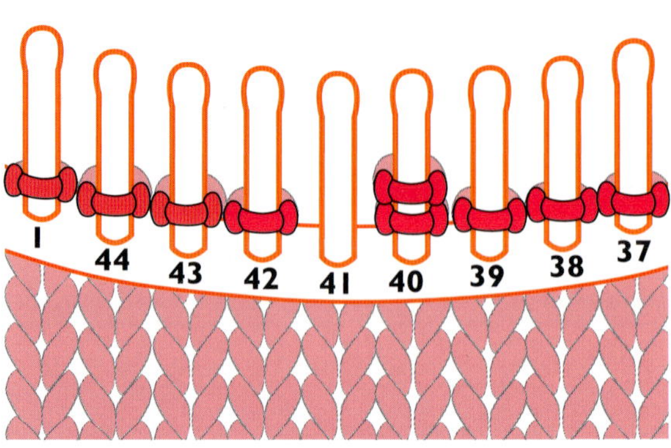

6 On the next row place the stitch on the third peg from the edge onto the fourth peg from the edge, and as you knit the row knit the 2 stitches as one. Then e-wrap the empty peg. This will create a buttonhole.

7 Knit 1 row. On the next row, bind (cast) off the 12 strap stitches and knit the rest of the row as normal. Knit 4 rows.

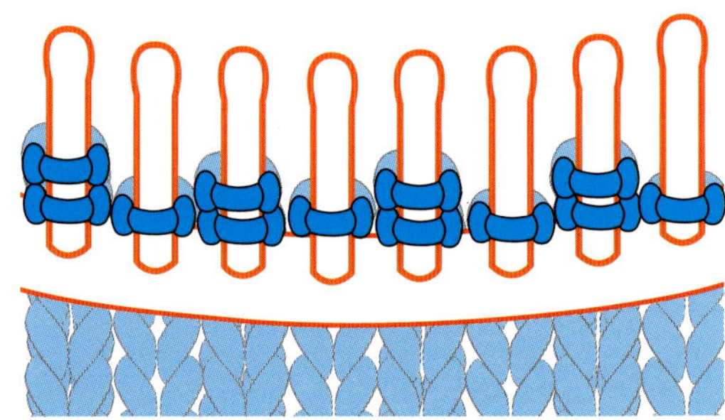

8 Decrease the Dusty Turquoise (A) section of the slipper by placing every third stitch onto the adjacent peg. Move all the stitches next to each other so there are no gaps. There will be 16 Dusty Turquoise (A) stitches remaining. Knit the row, treating each peg with 2 stitches as one stitch.

9 Cast on 10 stitches in Ruby (A) using the e-wrap technique (1 stitch on every other peg), so that you can knit the toe of the slipper.

10 Continue knitting backward and forward for 4 rows (not in the round) to keep the pattern of the stitches consistent. Twist the yarns together on each row when you change color so there are no holes.

11 Fasten off Ruby (B) and join in the second ball of Dusty Turquoise (A), so you have one ball for the front of the toe and one for the back. Continue to knit backward and forward in rows, remembering to twist the yarns on each row, for 2½in (6.5cm).

12 Decrease by placing every other stitch on the next peg, so there are 17 stitches. Knit for 2 rows. Work a gather bind (cast) off (see page 10). With right sides together, sew the seam at the back of the slipper keeping the seam as flat as possible so the slippers will be comfortable to wear.

13 Cover each button by sewing around the edge of the fabric circle with running stitch, then place a button in the center and pull on the thread ends to gather the fabric around the button. Push the back onto the button to secure the fabric. Sew a button to each slipper.

14 Stick a suede sole onto the bottom of each slipper, and add a sheepskin inner inside. Allow to dry. Sew in all the loose ends.

15 Repeat to make the second slipper, making sure you knit the strap from the other side in step 4.

Striped leg warmers

I love the bright colors in these stripy leg warmers. They're ideal for keeping little legs warm in the stroller.

YOU WILL NEED

- Stylecraft Special DK, 100% acrylic, light worsted (DK) yarn, 3½oz (100g) balls, approx. 322yds (295m) per ball:
  1 ball in each of Turquoise 1068 (A), Violet 1277 (B), Cream 1005 (C), Lime 1712 (D), Spice 1711 (E), and Fiesta 1257 (F)
- 4¾in (12cm) diameter round loom, with 44 pegs set ⅜in (9mm) apart
- US size E/4 (3.5mm) crochet hook
- Knitting tool
- Scissors
- Tapestry needle

SIZE

- Approx. 10in (25cm) long

INSTRUCTIONS

1 Cast on 44 stitches using Turquoise (A) and the cable cast on method (see page 8).

2 Work in k1, p1 rib for 12 rounds, and then knit 1 round.

3 Change to Cream (C) and knit 4 rounds. Change to Lime (D) and knit 12 rounds.

4 Repeat step 3, but instead of Lime (D) use Spice (E) and then Fiesta (F). Work another Cream (C) stripe, then change to Violet (B), and knit 1 round.

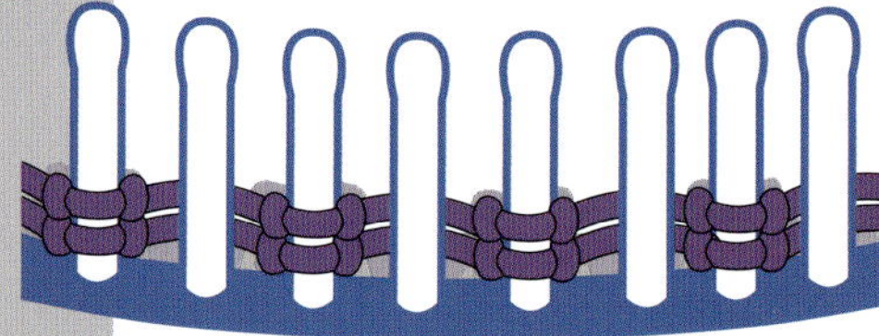

5 Decrease to 22 stitches, by placing alternate stitches on the next peg.

6 Work in k1, p1 rib for 5 rounds.

7 Bind (cast) off the first 11 stitches of the 22 stitches on the loom, then continue with k1, p1 rib for the remainder of the round.

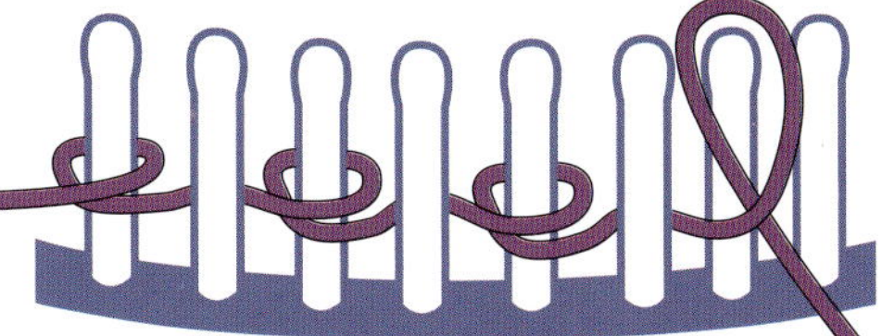

8 On the next round, e-wrap the first 11 pegs to replace the 11 stitches that you bound (cast) off on the round before.

9 Work in k1, p1 rib for 10 rounds. Bind (cast) off and sew in all the loose ends. Repeat to make the second leg warmer.

Gem headband

I adore the gem-encrusted glamour of this headband! It's made from super thick yarn so you can complete it in an evening.

YOU WILL NEED

- Lion Brand Wool Ease Thick & Quick, 86% acrylic/10% wool/4% rayon, super bulky (super chunky) yarn, 3½oz (100g) balls, approx. 106yds (97m) per ball: 1 ball of Grass 131
- 3½in (22cm) diameter round loom, with 72 pegs set ⅜in (9mm) apart
- US size E/4 (3.5mm) crochet hook
- Knitting tool
- Scissors
- Tapestry needle
- Assorted sew-on acrylic gems
- Sewing needle and lime green thread

SIZE

- Approx. 9in (22cm) wide (double for total width)

INSTRUCTIONS

1 Cast on 72 stitches using the cable cast on technique (see page 8).

2 Knit 3 rows, purl 7 rows. Repeat this sequence once more, then knit 3 rows.

3 Bind (cast) off.

4 Cast on 3 stitches using the e-wrap technique (see page 9).

5 Work garter stitch (knit 1 row, purl 1 row) for 25 rows.

6 Bind (cast) off, leaving a long yarn end.

7 Wrap this small strip around one side of the headband and sew the ends together using the yarn end.

8 To complete the headband, embellish the wrap band with the acrylic gems, sewing them on with the sewing needle and thread.

Panda pencil case

Create a fun furry panda pencil case to brighten up even the dreariest morning at school or work! By working the project in a purl stitch, the fluffy texture is emphasized.

YOU WILL NEED

- King Cole Cuddles Chunky, 100% polyester, bulky (chunky) yarn, 1¾oz (50g) balls, approx. 137yds (125m) per ball:
  1 ball each of Black 302 and White 350
- 8½in (22cm) long loom, with 52 pegs set ⅜in (9mm) apart
- Knitting tool
- Scissors
- Tapestry needle
- Pair of ¾ x ½in (18 x 13mm) cartoon toy safety eyes
- 10in (25cm) length of gingham ribbon
- Sewing needle and white thread
- 9½in (24cm) white zipper

SIZE

- Approx. 8½in (21cm) wide

INSTRUCTIONS

1 Start by making the ears: cast on 3 stitches using Black and the e-wrap technique (see page 9). Knit 2 rows.

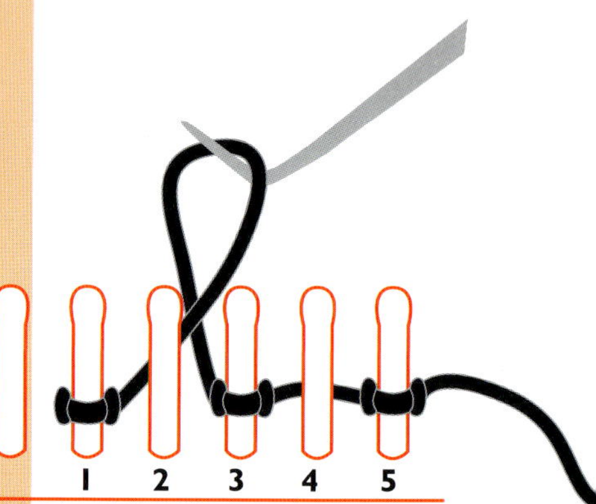

2 Increase twice on the next row, so move the stitch on the first peg to the next one on the left, pick up the bar of the stitch on the row below, twist, and place on the empty peg, then move the stitch on the last peg to the right, pick up the bar of the stitch on the row below, twist, and place on the empty peg. Knit 2 rows.

3 Repeat step 2, so there are now 7 stitches on the loom. Knit 3 rows.

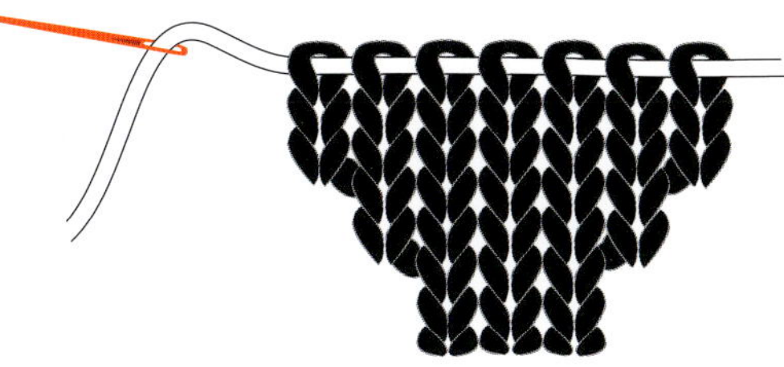

4 Thread a piece of waste yarn through the stitches and remove the ear from the loom. Repeat to make a second ear and put both to one side.

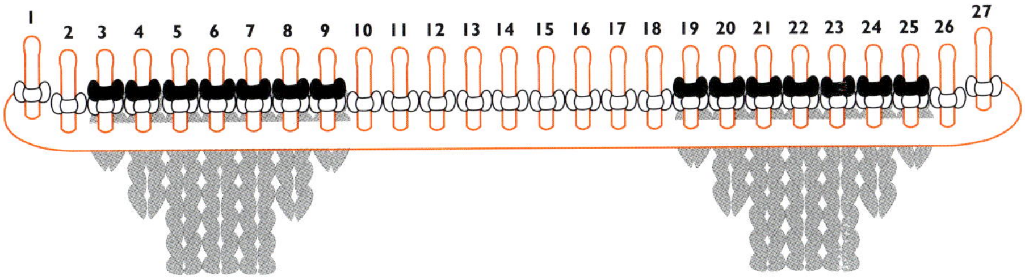

5 Cast on 52 stitches, using White and the e-wrap technique. Purl for 3 rows, or approximately ⅜in (1cm). Place the ears onto pegs 3 to 9 and 19 to 25, so they are facing outward. Hook the bottom White stitch over the Black ones to secure the ears in place.

6 Purl in white for 1¼in (3cm), or approximately 9 rows. Wind 2 small balls of Black, with approximately 2⅛yds (2m) of yarn in each. Attach one using a slip knot to stitch 9 and the other to stitch 17.

7 Purl stitches 9 and 10 and stitches 17 and 18 using Black, and purl all the other stitches in that row in White. Remember to twist the yarns together when changing color to avoid a hole in the knitting.

8 Repeat step 7 for 2 more rows.

9 For the next 3 rows, knit Black on stitches 8 to 11 and 16 to 19, and White on all the rest. For the next 3 rows, purl Black on stitches 7 to 11 and 16 to 20, and White on all the rest.
For the next 5 rows, purl Black on stitches 6 to 10 and 19 to 21, and White on all the rest.
For the next 3 rows, purl Black on stitches 7 to 10 and 18 to 21, and White on all the rest.
For the next 3 rows, purl Black on stitches 7 to 9 and 19 to 21, and White on all the rest.
Cut Black from the back of the work, leaving a 4in (10cm) tail to be sewn in at a later stage.

10 Purl for 2 rows in White.

11 Join one of the balls of Black to stitch 12 using a slip knot, and purl stitches 12 to 14 in Black and the rest in White for 3 rows.
Purl in white for 1¼in (3cm), or approximately 9 rows.

12 Place stitches 1 to 26 on a length of waste thread, then take them across and place them on the corresponding peg opposite (so stitch 1 on peg 52, stitch 2 on peg 51, and so on).

13 Bind (cast) off, and then sew in all the loose ends.

14 Add the cartoon eyes onto the black eye areas, securing in place with the backs.

15 Using backstitch (see page 16) and Black, sew a mouth down from the nose.

16 Tie a bow in the ribbon and sew it to the ear with a few stitches in white thread.

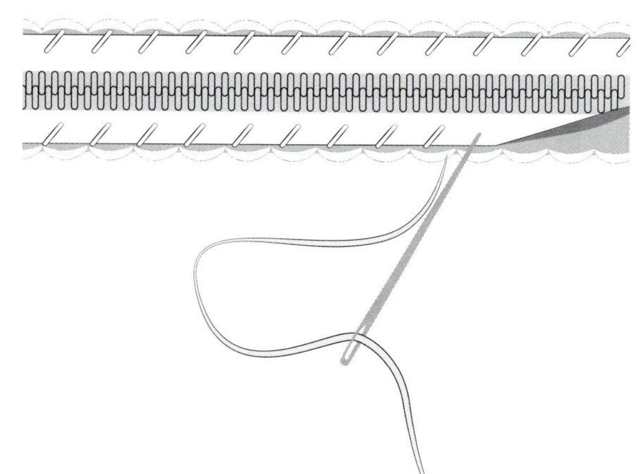

17 Finally, turn the pencil case inside out and sew the zipper into the opening in the knitted piece.

Jungle finger puppets

Your little ones will love these delightful jungle characters! Made from small scraps of yarn, they are a great stash buster so you can use up all your leftover yarns.

YOU WILL NEED

- 100% cotton DK (light worsted) yarn, or similar: 7/8oz (25g) each of mustard yellow, dark orange, light gray, brown, and beige
- 7¼ x 2in (18 x 5cm) sock loom, with pegs set ¼in (6mm) apart
- US size E/4 (3.5mm) crochet hook
- Knitting tool
- Scissors
- Tapestry needle
- Black seed beads
- Scrap of dark cream felt
- Needle and cream thread
- Dark pink stranded embroidery floss
- Scrap of coral felt
- Scrap of brown felt
- Toy stuffing

SIZE

- Approx. 4¾in (12cm) tall

INSTRUCTIONS

LION

1 Using mustard yellow, cast on 16 stitches using the cable cast on technique (see page 8). Knit for 35 rounds.

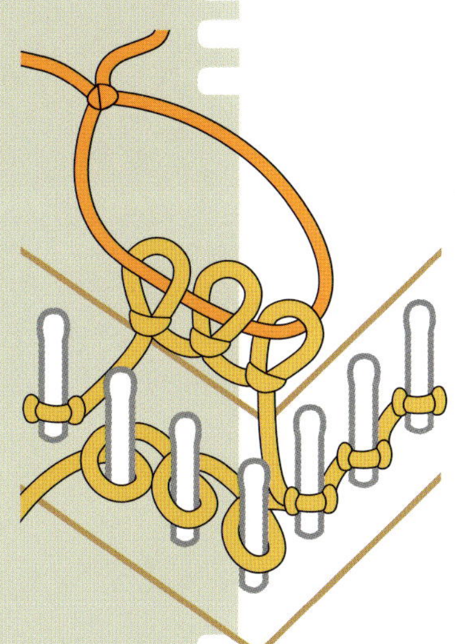

2 To make the armholes, thread stitches 1 to 3 and 9 to 11 onto a piece of waste yarn and remove from the loom. E-wrap the empty pegs.

3 Knit 2 rounds.

4 On the next round, increase by 2 stitches, once on peg 4 and once on peg 13, so there are now 18 stitches on the loom. Knit 1 round.

5 On the next round, increase by 2 stitches, once on peg 1 and once on peg 9, so there are 20 stitches on the loom. Knit 1 round.

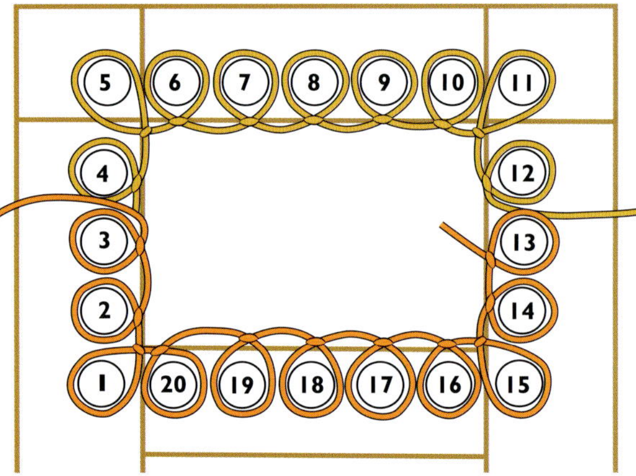

6 On the following round, knit stitches 1 to 12 in mustard yellow, then attach the dark orange yarn on stitch 13, and knit the rest of the round and the first 3 stitches of the next round in dark orange.

7 Knit stitches 12 back to 3 in mustard yellow. Twist the mustard yellow and dark orange yarns together.

8 Start knitting the dark orange section in loopy stitch: wrap dark orange around peg 3 three times, then hook the bottom loop over the top 3 wraps.

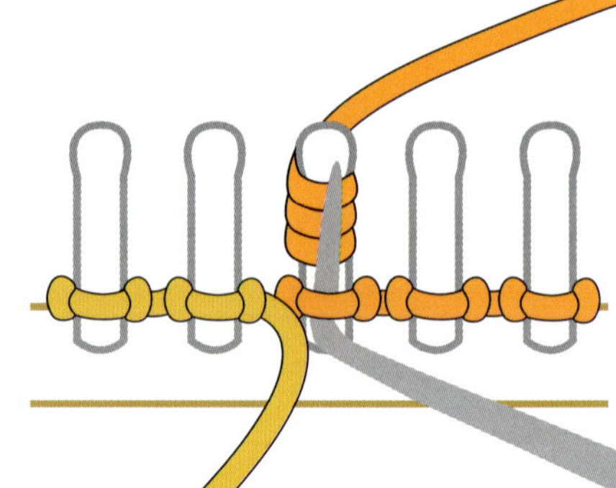

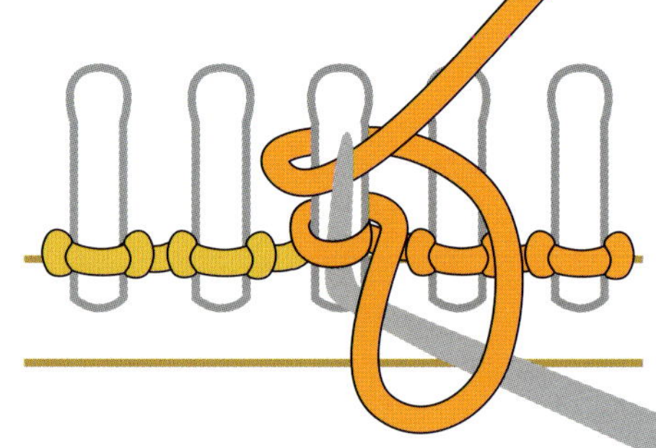

9 Pull off the top 2 wraps and move to one side of the peg. Leave the third stitch on the peg as a "stitch." Then knit this "stitch" twice to secure.

10 Work loop stitch to stitch 13 in dark orange. Then knit in mustard yellow back to stitch 12, twist the ends together, and knit the dark orange section, not looping this time.

11 Repeat steps 8 to 10 six more times.

12 Using dark orange only, loop knit the whole way around the head. Knit 1 round.

13 Repeat knit 2 stitches together, k2 around the loom, so there are 15 stitches left on the loom. Loop knit the next row. Knit 1 round.
Work a gather bind (cast) off (see page 10).

14 Place a small ball of toy stuffing up into the head. Using a piece of mustard yarn and the tapestry needle, sew small running stitches (see page 16) around the neck and pull tight, before knotting and sewing the ends into the head to hide them.

15 To make the arms, place the 3 stitches on the waste yarn on the loom, and the 3 e-wrapped stitches. Knit across these 6 stitches for 12 rounds in mustard yellow. Gather bind (cast) off. Repeat for second arm.

16 Sew on 2 beads for the eyes. Cut the face from cream felt, using the template on page 124, and sew onto the face. To complete your lion, backstitch (see page 16) a mouth and nose onto the felt section, using dark pink embroidery floss and following the photo as a guide.

ELEPHANT

1 Using light gray, repeat steps 1 to 5 of the Lion, then knit 2 more rounds. On the next round, place stitches 7 to 9 onto a piece of waste yarn and e-wrap the empty pegs. This will eventually become the trunk.

2 Knit for 10 rows. Repeat knit 2 stitches together, knit 2 around the loom, so there are 15 stitches. Knit 1 row. Work a gather bind (cast) off (see page 10).

3 Place a small ball of toy stuffing up into the head. Using a piece of light gray yarn and the tapestry needle, sew small running stitches (see page 16) around the neck and pull tight, before knotting and sewing the ends into the head to hide them.

4 Using light gray, knit the arms and the trunk as per the arms in step 15 of the Lion.

5 Using light gray, make the ears by casting on 14 stitches, and knitting for 12 rows. Work a gather bind (cast) off. Repeat to make the second ear. Stitch to the side of the head.

6 Sew on 2 beads for the eyes. Cut the nose from coral felt, using the template on page 124, and sew to the end of the trunk.

MONKEY

1 Using brown, repeat steps 1 to 5 of the Lion, but as well as making armholes on round 36 (step 2), work step 2 on round 5 to make holes for the legs, and also on this round thread stitches 13 to 15 onto a piece of waste yarn and remove from the loom to make a hole for the tail.

2 To make the head, repeat steps 4 and 5 once more so there are 24 stitches on the head. Knit 4 rounds.

3 Knit 2 stitches together, k10, knit 2 stitches together, k10, so there are 22 stitches in the round. Knit 1 round.

4 K9, knit 2 stitches together, k9, knit 2 stitches together, so there are 20 stitches in the round. Knit 1 round.

5 Knit 2 stitches together, k8, knit 2 stitches together, k8, so there are 18 stitches in the round. Knit 1 round.

6 K7, knit 2 stitches together, k7, knit 2 stitches together, so there are 16 stitches in the round. Knit 1 round.

7 Work a gather bind (cast) off (see page 10).

8 Place a small ball of toy stuffing up into the head. Using a piece of brown yarn and the tapestry needle, sew small running stitches (see page 16) around the neck and pull tight, before knotting and sewing the ends into the head to hide them.

9 Make the legs and arms as in step 15 of the Lion, beginning with brown for the first 9 rounds, then changing to beige for the last 3 rounds. Work a gather bind (cast) off. Make the tail in the same way, but using only brown and knitting 18 rounds.

10 Sew on 2 beads for the eyes. Cut the ears from brown felt, and the face from cream felt, using the templates on page 124. Sew the ears on either side of the head, and the face onto the front of the head. Backstitch (see page 16) a mouth in dark pink embroidery floss to complete.

Baby activity block

This textured block shows off your knitting skills, as well as being a really personal baby gift. If you are feeling adventurous, make a set of them and add numbers, letters, and other decoration using colored felt.

YOU WILL NEED

- Rico Creative Cotton DK, 100% cotton, light worsted (DK) yarn, 1¾oz (50g) balls, approx. 126yds (115m) per ball: 1 ball each of Light Yellow 003, Orange 007, Red 008, Cardinal 010, Royal Blue 012, and Pistachio 016
- 7¼ x 2in (18 x 5cm) sock loom, with 60 pegs set ¼in (6mm) apart
- Knitting tool
- Scissors
- Tapestry needle
- 2in (5cm) thick upholstery foam cut into two 4in (10cm) squares

SIZE

- Each side measures approx. 4in (10cm)

INSTRUCTIONS

1 Using Red, cast on 20 stitches using the e-wrap technique (see page 9).

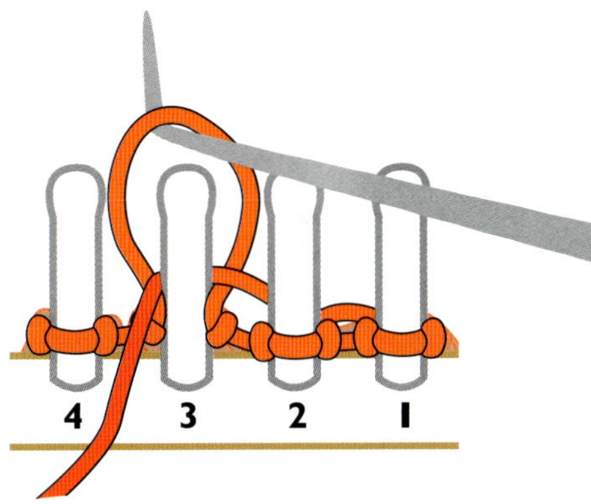

2 You'll work the first section in bamboo stitch: For row 1, skip the first stitch (the first stitch of every row is slipped for a neat edge), then repeat knit 2, purl 1 to the last peg.
For row 2, skip the first stitch, then repeat purl 1, knit 2 to the last peg, knit the last stitch.
For row 3, skip the first stitch. Bring the yarn to the front of the next 2 stitches by lifting the stitches off the peg one at a time and placing the working yarn behind the peg, knit 1. Repeat this sequence to the last peg, knit the last stitch.

3 For row 4, skip the first stitch, then repeat purl 1, knit 2 to the last peg, knit the last stitch.

4 Repeat rows 1 to 4 (steps 2 and 3) for 52 more rows.

5 Continue skipping the first stitch of every row from now on. For the next row, change to Royal Blue yarn and repeat knit 2, purl 2 along the row.

6 Attach the Light Yellow yarn to peg 21 and cast on 20 stitches using the e-wrap technique.

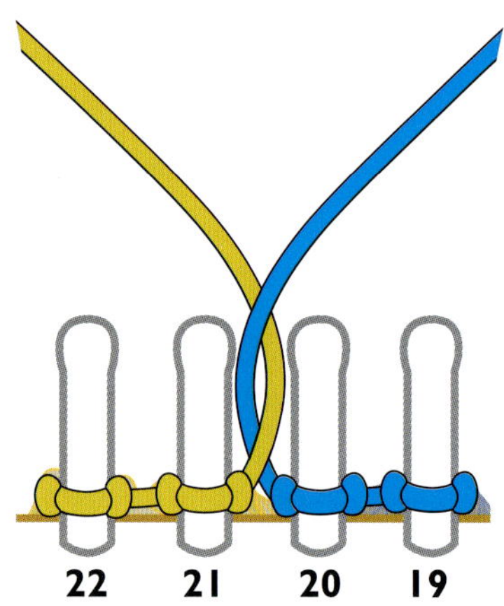

7 For the next 42 rows, work in k2, p2 rib on the Royal Blue section (Row 1: purl 2, knit 2, Row 2: knit 2, purl 2) and on the Light Yellow section repeat 5 rows of knit, followed by 1 row of purl. Finish with 3 rows of rib on the Royal Blue section and 3 rows of knit on the Light Yellow section. Twist the yarns together where they meet to ensure there is no hole.

8 Bind (cast) off the 20 Light Yellow stitches.

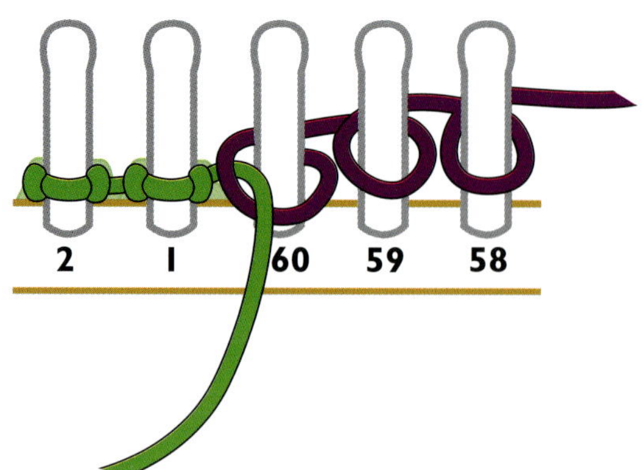

9 Fasten off the Royal Blue yarn, and change to Pistachio on this section. Knit one row. Attach the Cardinal yarn to the peg to the right of the Pistachio, and cast on 20 stitches using the e-wrap technique.

10 For the next 45 rows, knit every row on the Pistachio section and work garter stitch (1 row knit, 1 row purl) on the Cardinal section. Make sure you twist the ends around each other where they meet.

11 Bind (cast) off the Cardinal section.

12 Change the Pistachio to Orange yarn and work double seed (moss) stitch:
For rows 1 and 2, repeat knit 1, purl 1 to the end of the row.
For rows 3 and 4, repeat purl 1, knit 1 to the end of the row.

13 Work 44 more rows, then bind (cast) off.

14 Place two pieces of foam on top of one another and stretch the knitted piece around the block. Stitch in place using the yarn and tapestry needle.

Toddler's chunky poncho

This chunky knit poncho is easy to make, super snug, and stylish too. Wooden buttons complete the look.

YOU WILL NEED

- Drops Andes, 65% wool/35% alpaca, super bulky (chunky) yarn, 3½oz (100g) balls, approx. 85yds (75m) per ball: 4 balls of Light Sea Green 9023
- 21in (53cm) long loom, with 62 pegs set ¾in (18mm) apart
- Knitting tool
- Scissors
- Tapestry needle
- 4 x wooden buttons, ⅞in (2cm) diameter

SIZE

- To fit age 2–4 years, 16½in (42cm) wide (laid flat) x 19in (48cm) long (shoulder to hem)

INSTRUCTIONS

1 Cast on 55 stitches using the e-wrap technique (see page 9).

2 For row 1, skip the first stitch (the first stitch of every row is slipped for a neat edge), k4, repeat k1, p1 for 44 stitches, k6. For row 2, repeat row 1.

3 For row 3, skip the first stitch, p4, repeat k1, p1 for 44 stitches, k1, p5. For row 4, repeat row 3.

4 Repeat rows 1 to 4 three times.

5 For rows 17 and 18, skip the first stitch, knit the row.

6 For rows 19 and 20, skip the first stitch, p4, k45, p5.

7 Repeat rows 17 to 20 for a further 76 rows. You can work more rows for a taller child or fewer rows for a shorter one.

8 For the next row, skip the first stitch, k19, then thread a length of waste yarn through the next 15 stitches and remove them from the loom. E-wrap the empty pegs and then knit the remaining 20 stitches.

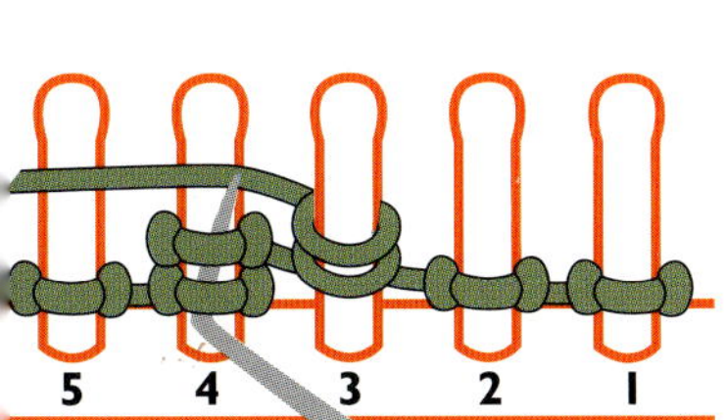

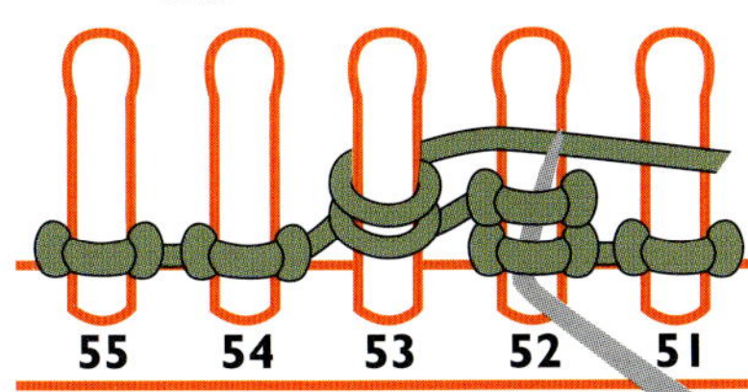

9 Repeat steps 8 to 2 in reverse to make the other half of the poncho, but on rows 60 and 80 make two buttonholes: for the first buttonhole move stitch 3 onto peg 4, e-wrap the empty peg 3 twice and knit both stitches on peg 4 as one stitch. For the second buttonhole at the other end of each of these rows, move stitch 53 onto peg 52, knit both stitches on peg 52 as one stitch and double e-wrap peg 53.

10 Bind (cast) off and sew in all of the ends. Sew the wooden buttons in place to match the position of the buttonholes.

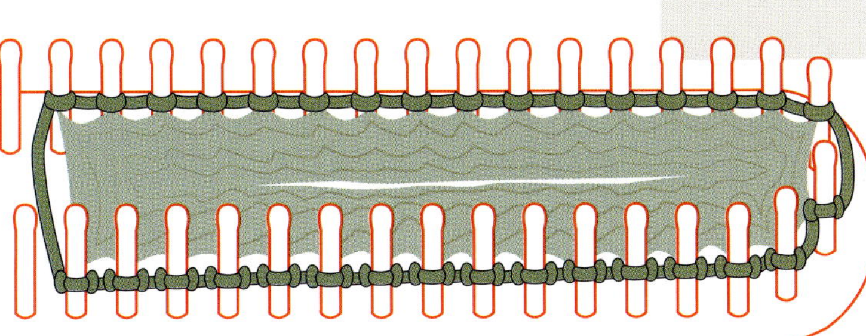

11 To make the collar, place the 15 stitches on the waste yarn and the 15 e-wrapped cast-on stitches back onto one end of the loom, to create a small round.

12 Work in k1, p1 rib for 20 rounds. Using your hook, pull up the first stitches that you placed on the loom in step 14 back onto the pegs, and hook over so that the folded collar is secured in place.

13 Bind (cast) off loosely so that it is not too tight when you are pulling over the head.

CHAPTER FOUR

Home Accessories

Knotted coasters

These knotted coasters are made from a gorgeous variegated yarn that looks fabulous once its twisted into shape. Add a felt back to each coaster to hide all the stitches that keep them held together!

YOU WILL NEED

- Rico Creative Melange DK, 53% wool/47% acrylic, light worsted (DK) yarn, 1¾oz (50g) balls, approx. 98yds (90m) per ball: 1 ball of Purple-Teal 021
- 1in (2.5cm) diameter round loom, with 5 pegs set ¾in (18mm) apart
- Knitting tool
- Scissors
- Tapestry needle
- 4 pink felt circles, each approx. 4in (10cm) diameter
- Sewing needle and pink thread

SIZE

- Approx. 4in (10cm) diameter

INSTRUCTIONS

1 Cast on 5 stitches using the e-wrap technique (see page 9), and knit for 60in (150cm).

2 Work the gather bind (cast) off method (see page 10), and sew in all the loose ends.

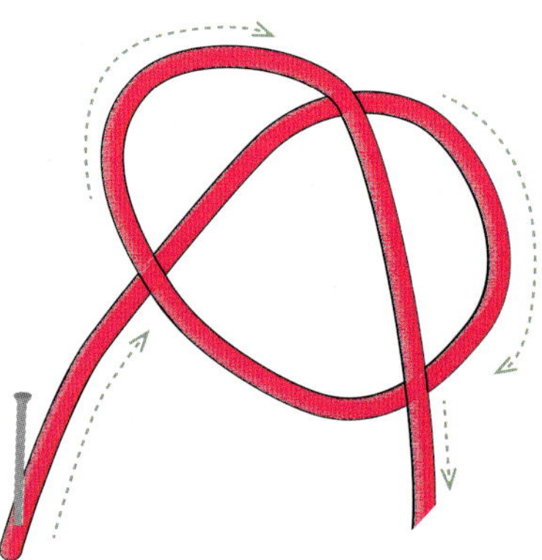

3 Pin one end of the cord to a surface such as the carpet, then loop it round as shown in the illustration.

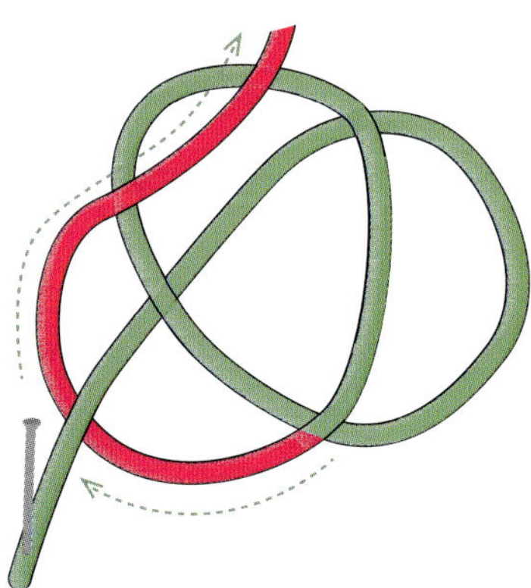

4 Thread the cord under and over the first part of the knot.

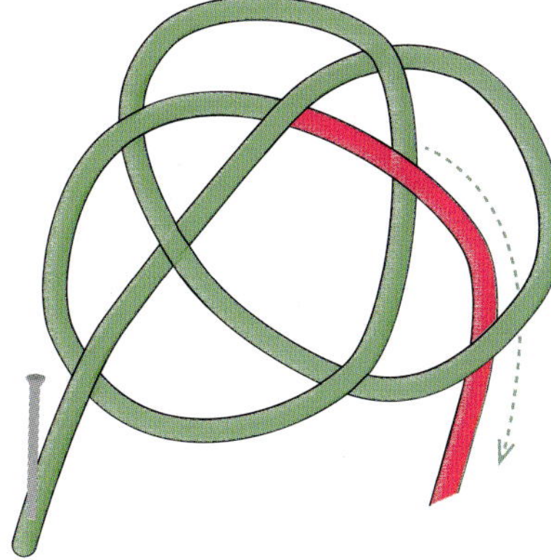

5 Thread the cord under, over, and under the knot as shown.

6 To thicken the knot, thread the remaining cord through the knot again in the same way as in steps 3 to 5.

7 Turn the knot over, take the ends round following the design, and sew them to the back. Add a few stitches to hold the knot in place.

8 Sew the felt circle to the back of the coaster to neaten. Repeat the steps to make 3 more coasters.

Retro throw pillow

These squares are wrapped around the loom rather than knitted, but this creates a fab alternative to a crochet pillow.

YOU WILL NEED

- Stylecraft Special DK, 100% acrylic, light worsted (DK) yarn, 3½oz (100g) balls, approx. 322yds (295m) per ball: 1 ball each of Violet 1277 (A), Empire 1829 (B), Fuchsia Purple 1827 (C), Silver 1203 (D), and Midnight 1011 (E)
- Square flower loom
- Tapestry needle
- US size E/4 (3.5mm) crochet hook
- 2 x 19in (48cm) squares of fabric
- Sewing needle and white thread
- Scissors
- 18in (46cm) square pillow form

SIZE

- 18in (46cm) square

INSTRUCTIONS

1 Using Violet (A), make a slip knot and place it on the third peg along from the bottom left corner.

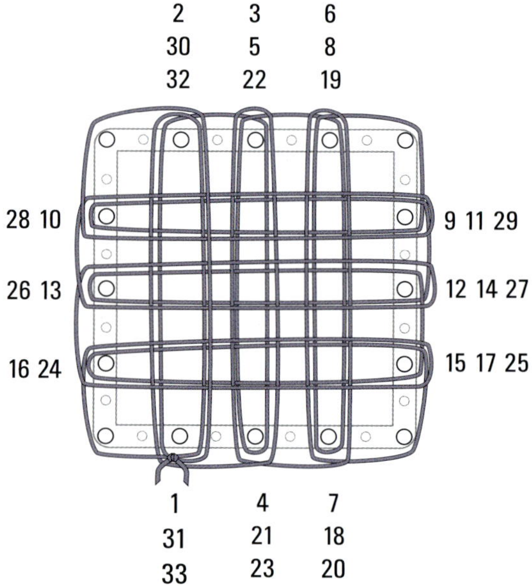

2 Wrap the loom in the numbered order shown in the illustration.

3 Repeat step 2 two more times, then tie the working yarn end to the slip knot end to secure.

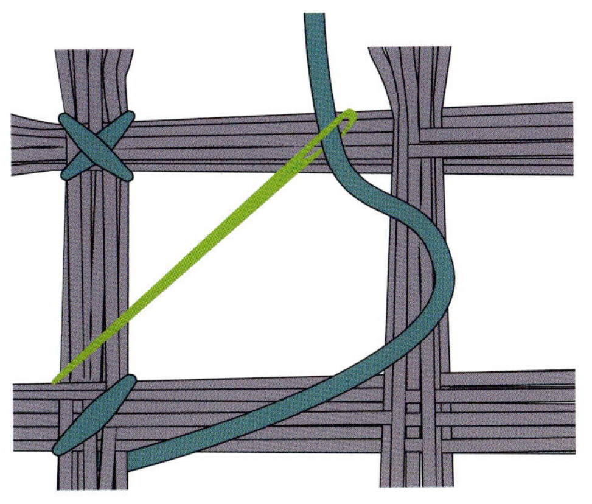

4 Cut a length of Empire (B) and thread it onto the tapestry needle. Work a cross stitch where one set of yarn strands cross on the grid, tying the yarn end to the working yarn to secure it. Then take the working yarn behind the wraps to work a cross stitch at the next junction.

5 Repeat on all the other junctions of the grid, then tie off the yarn neatly at the end.

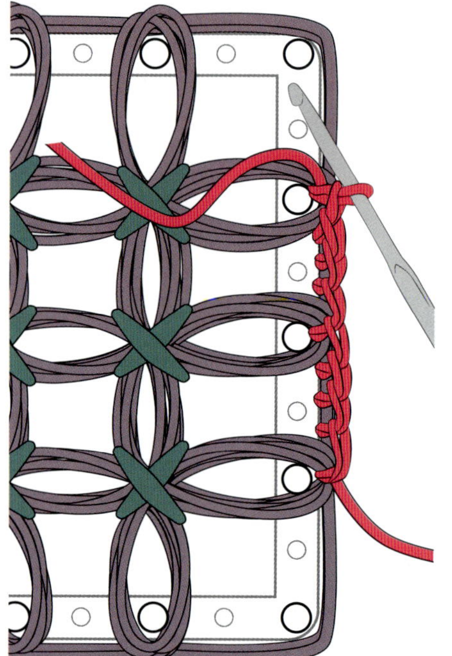

6 With the yarn grid still on the loom, work single (UK double) crochet stitches (see page 15) all around the edge using Fuchsia Purple (C), working 9 stitches in each corner–one in each loop of yarn–and 3 stitches along the strands between each loop.

7 Slip the work off the loom and then work another round of single (UK double) crochet, making 1 stitch into each stitch along the sides and 3 stitches into each corner stitch.

8 Repeat steps 1 to 7 three more times, to make 4 squares in total.

9 Then make a second set of 4 squares using Fuchsia Purple (C) to wrap, with Violet (A) cross stitches, and Silver (D) crochet.

10 Make a third set of 4 squares using Empire (B) to wrap, with Silver (D) cross stitches and Violet (A) crochet, and finally 4 squares with Silver (D) wraps, Fuchsia Purple (C) cross stitches, and Empire (B) crochet.

11 Using the photograph as a guide for positioning, use a single (UK double) crochet seam (see page 15) and Midnight (E) to join the squares together into one large square. Work a round of single (UK double) crochet all around the edge of the joined squares in Midnight (E), then 1 round in Empire (B), 1 round in Fuchsia Purple (C), 1 round in Silver (D), and 1 round in Violet (A).

12 Press the square with a steam iron to block to a square shape and the finished size.

13 Place the two pieces of fabric right sides together and sew around 3 sides using backstitch (see page 16), taking a ½in (12mm) seam allowance.

14 Turn the fabric pocket right side out, press, and insert the pillow form. Fold under the raw edges and sew the open side closed.

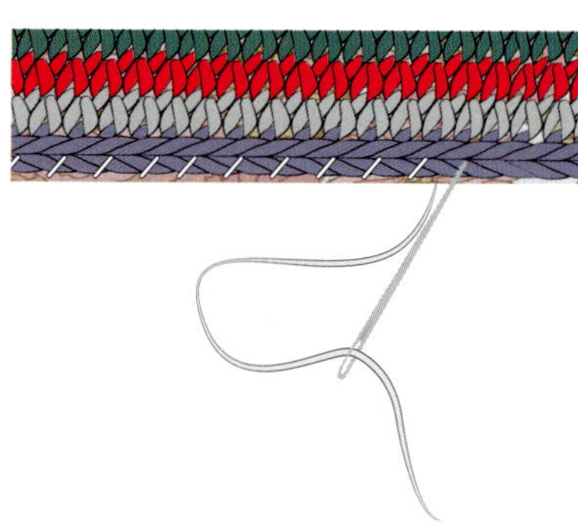

15 Place the squares panel on one side of the pillow and sew them together all around the edge to complete.

Hanging potholder

Macramé potholders are so stylish at the moment, and with this pattern you can create your own loom-knitted version. Try hanging one in the bathroom, or hang in groups for a fantastic effect.

YOU WILL NEED

- 11oz (300g) of ⅛in (3mm) cream cord
- 4¾in (12cm) diameter round loom, with 24 pegs set ¾in (18mm) apart
- Knitting tool
- Tapestry needle
- 4¾in x 1in (12 x 2.5cm) piece of cardstock
- Sewing needle and white thread
- Scissors
- 5½in (14cm) long x 4¾in (12cm) diameter metal pot

SIZE

- Approx. 20in (50cm) long, without tassel

INSTRUCTIONS

1 Make a slip knot and place it on the first peg of the loom. Cast on 24 stitches, using the e-wrap technique (see page 9).

2 Number the first peg as 1, and the next 2 pegs to the right as 2 and 3, as shown in the illustration.

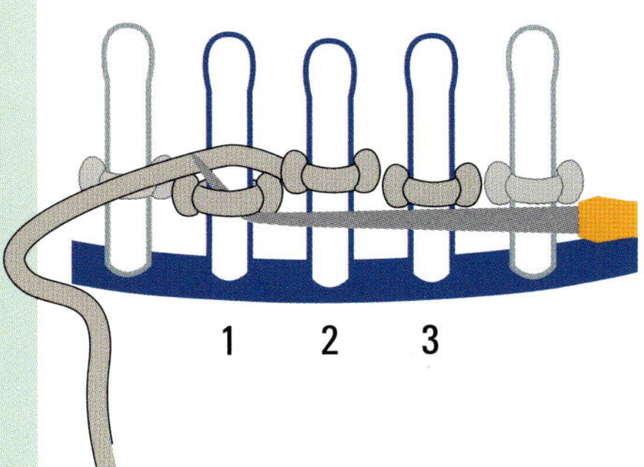

3 Knit the stitch on peg 1.

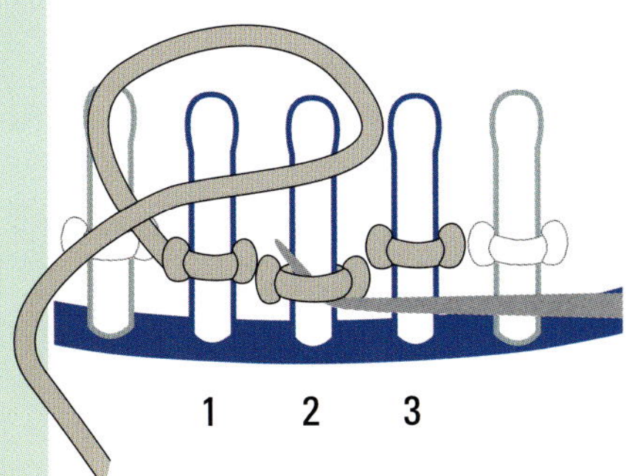

4 Take the yarn around both pegs and knit the stitches on pegs 2 and 1.

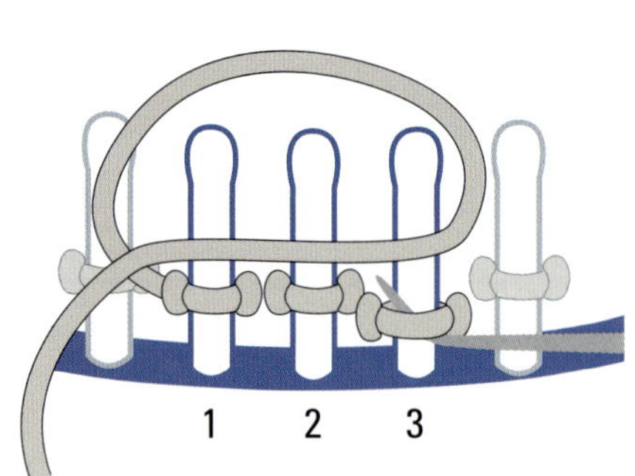

5 Take the yarn around all 3 pegs and knit the stitches on pegs 3, 2, and 1.

6 Steps 3 to 5 complete the stitch sequence. Renumber the pegs one step to the left, so peg 1 becomes peg 2, the peg to its left becomes peg 1, and peg 2 becomes peg 3. Repeat the stitch sequence on these 3 pegs.

7 Continue knitting in rounds in this way, until the piece is 5½in (14cm) long.

8 Now decrease, by placing alternate stitches onto the next peg along so there are 2 stitches on every other peg. Knit 2 rounds.

9 Bind (cast) off, using the gather bind (cast) off method (see page 10).

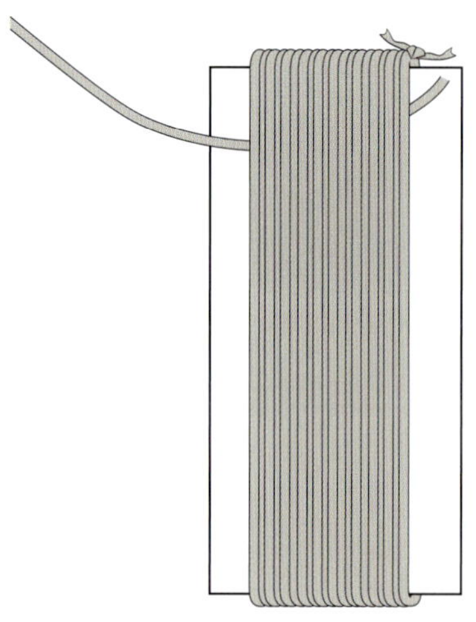

10 Make a tassel by wrapping cord lengthwise around the piece of cardstock 20 times. Thread a 8in (20cm) piece of the cord through the loops.

11 Tie the short length of cord into a tight knot at the top of the loops. Remove the cardstock and wrap another piece of cord around the neck of the tassel, pulling it tight and then threading the loose ends down through the tassel to secure. Unravel the cord ends to make a bushier tassel.

12 Sew or tie the tassel to the bottom of the potholder.

13 Cut nine lengths of cord 60in (1.5m) long. Thread 3 of them through a suitable gap in the top edge of the potholder, fold in half and then braid (plait) the cords—there will be 2 cords in each bunch of the braid.

14 Repeat with the other 2 bunches of 3 cords, spacing them evenly apart around the pot holder so there are 3 braided cords coming off the top edge.

15 Loop the 3 braid ends into a ring and then wrap around them with cord and then around the neck to create a hanging loop. Sew the wraps in place securely with the sewing needle and thread. Push the pot into the potholder and it's ready to add a potted plant.

Jute storage basket

Worked in a combination of stitches to give a basketweave pattern on the sides, this pretty two-color container is ideal for storing all kinds of small things.

YOU WILL NEED

- 55yds (50m) spool of jute yarn in turquoise (A)
- 110yds (100m) spool of jute yarn in natural (B)
- 8½in (22cm) long knitting loom, with 56 pegs set ⅜in (9mm) apart
- US size E/4 (3.5mm) crochet hook
- Knitting tool
- Tapestry needle
- Scissors

SIZE

- Approx. 6in (15cm) at widest point

INSTRUCTIONS

1 Make a slip knot with the turquoise jute (A) and place it on the first peg of the loom. Cast on 56 stitches using the cable cast on technique (see page 8).

2 For the first round, knit all around the loom.

3 For rounds 2, 3, and 4 repeat p5, k3 all the way around the loom.

4 For round 5, knit all around the loom.

5 For rounds 6, 7, and 8 repeat p1, k3, p5 all the way around the loom.

6 Repeat steps 2 to 5 three more times.

7 Change to natural jute (B) and repeat steps 2 to 5 twice.

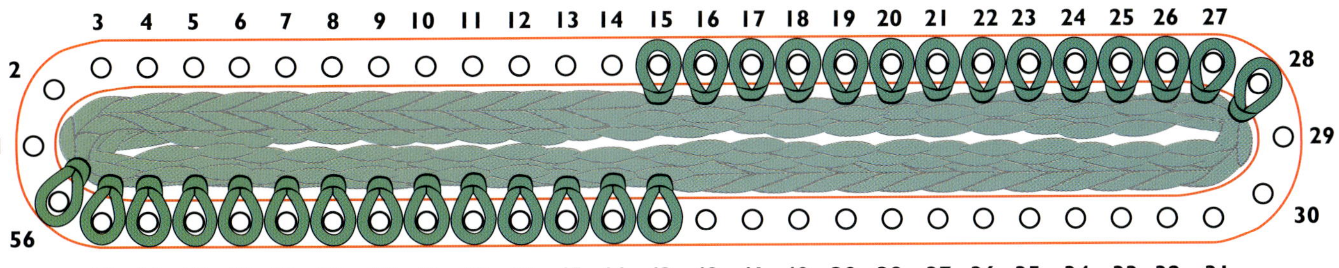

8 Bind (cast) off stitches 1 to 14, knit stitches 15 to 28, bind (cast) off stitches 29 to 42, and leave stitches 43 to 56 on the loom but don't knit them.

9 For the bottom of the basket, continue knitting stitches 15 to 28 backward and forward in rows until this piece measures the same as the height of the basket (approximately 4in/10cm).

10 Hook the stitches on pegs 15 to 28 onto pegs 56 to 43, ensuring they match up straight, and bind (cast) off them off together to join the bottom to the sides along one edge.

11 Sew up the other two side seams on either side of the bottom panel to complete.

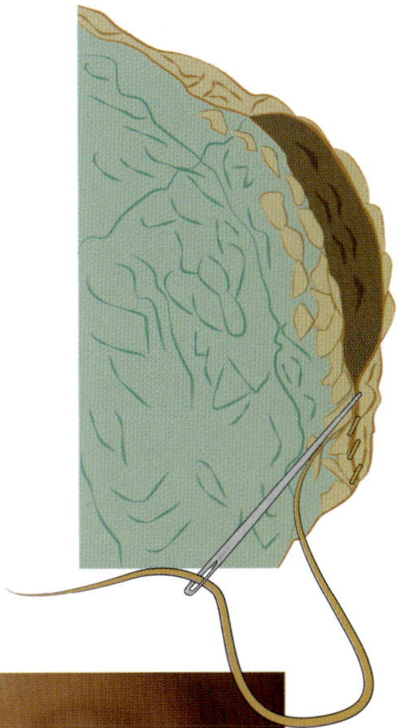

Fox storage jar

Cheer up your shelves with this cute fox storage jar. Ideal for the kitchen or craft room, you'll never have naked jars again!

YOU WILL NEED

- Drops Baby Merino, 100% wool, sportweight (lightweight DK) yarn, 1¾oz (50g) balls, approx. 191yds (175m) per ball: 1 ball of Electric Orange 36
- Scraps of black yarn
- 7¼ x 2in (18 x 5cm) sock loom, with 60 pegs set ¼in (6mm) apart
- US size E/4 (3.5mm) crochet hook
- Knitting tool
- Scissors
- Tapestry needle
- 2 x green buttons, ½in (12mm) diameter
- Cream felt
- Black felt

SIZE

- Approx. 4¾in (12cm) diameter (across open edge) x 4in (10cm) tall

INSTRUCTIONS

1 Start by making the ears. Cast on 2 stitches on pegs 8 and 9. Work garter stitch (knit 1 row, purl 1 row) for 4 rows. Move the stitch on peg 9 to peg 10.

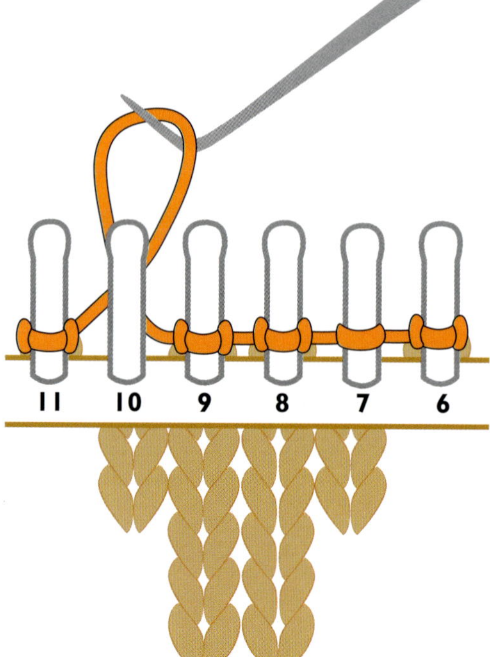

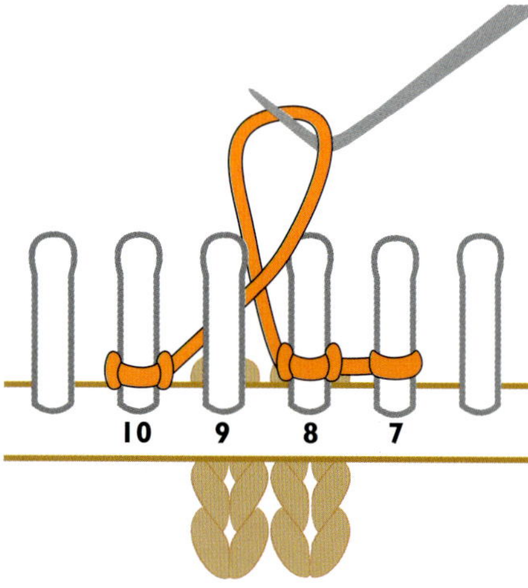

2 Pick up the loop at the end of the row, twist, and place on peg 7. Then pick up the bar of the stitch between pegs 10 and 8, twist, and place on peg 9.

3 Work garter stitch for 6 rows. Move stitch 7 onto peg 6 and stitch 10 onto peg 11. Pick up the bars of the stitches below, twist, and place on the empty pegs.

4 Work garter stitch for 2 rows. Cut the yarn, leaving a long tail.

5 Cast on 2 stitches on pegs 17 and 18. Work garter stitch for 4 rows. Move the stitch on peg 18 to peg 19. Pick up the bar of the stitch between pegs 17 and 19 and place it on peg 18. Then pick up the loop at the end of the row and place it on peg 16. Work garter stitch for 6 rows. Move stitch 16 onto peg 15 and stitch 19 onto peg 20. Pick up the bars of the stitches below, twist, and place on the empty pegs.
Repeat step 4.

6 Attach the yarn on peg 1 and cast on one stitch on every peg, knitting across each ear as you come to it, until all 60 pegs have stitches. Work garter stitch for 40 rounds.

7 Begin to reduce the piece by knitting 2 stitches together on pegs 25 and 55. Move the stitches down by one on each side and reduce the size of the loom to 58 stitches. Work garter stitch for 2 rounds.

8 Reduce the piece again by knitting 2 stitches together on pegs 1 and 29. Move the stitches down by one on each side and reduce the size of the loom to 56 stitches.

9 Repeat steps 6 and 7, alternating the corners that the stitches are reduced on, until there are only 34 stitches on the loom.

10 Knit 4, then repeat knit 2 stitches together, knit 1 to the end of the round, so there are now 24 stitches on the loom. Knit 2 rounds of garter stitch.

11 Repeat knit 2 stitches together, knit 1 to the end of the round, so that there are now 16 stitches on the loom. Knit 2 rounds of garter stitch.

12 Work a gather bind (cast) off (see page 10).

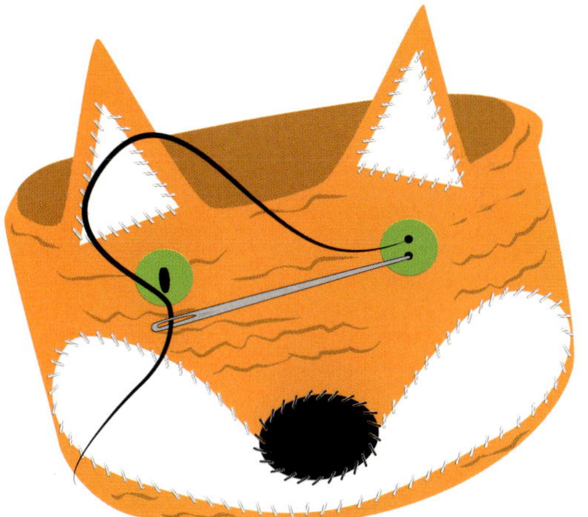

13 Using the templates on page 122, cut out the cheeks and two ears from the cream felt and a nose from the black felt. Stitch onto the face. Add green buttons for the eyes.

14 Complete by working single (UK double) crochet (see page 15) or blanket stitch (see page 17) around the ears, using the black yarn.

Basketweave lampshade

This open-weave knit stitch is perfect for a lampshade, because the light will still filter through. You may need to adapt the pattern slightly to fit your particular shade.

YOU WILL NEED

- Paintbox Yarns Wool Blend Super Chunky, 75% acrylic/25% wool, super bulky (super chunky) yarn, 3½oz (100g) balls, approx. 66yds (60m) per ball: 1 ball of Magenta Pink 15
- 6¼in (16cm) diameter round loom, with 32 pegs set ¾in (18mm) apart
- US size E/4 (3.5mm) crochet hook
- Knitting tool
- Scissors
- Tapestry needle
- Sewing needle and purple thread
- 9½in (23cm) tall x 5in (13cm) diameter lampshade

SIZE

- Approx. 9½in (23cm) tall

INSTRUCTIONS

1 Cast on 32 stitches using the cable cast on technique (see page 8).

2 Work every round knit stitch for 5 rounds.

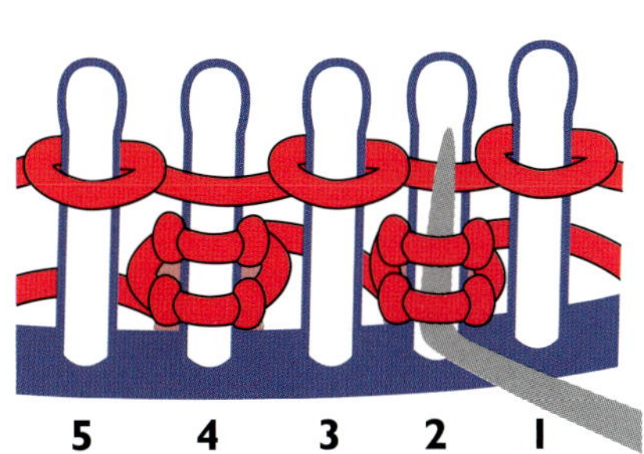

3 For round 6, move the odd stitches onto the even pegs all the way around the loom. E-wrap the empty pegs and knit the two stitches on the even pegs as one.

4 On rounds 7 to 9, repeat p2, k1, p1 around the loom.

5 For round 10, repeat round 1.

6 On rounds 11 to 13, repeat k1, p3, around the loom.

7 Repeat rounds 6 to 13 three more times.

8 Bind (cast) off.

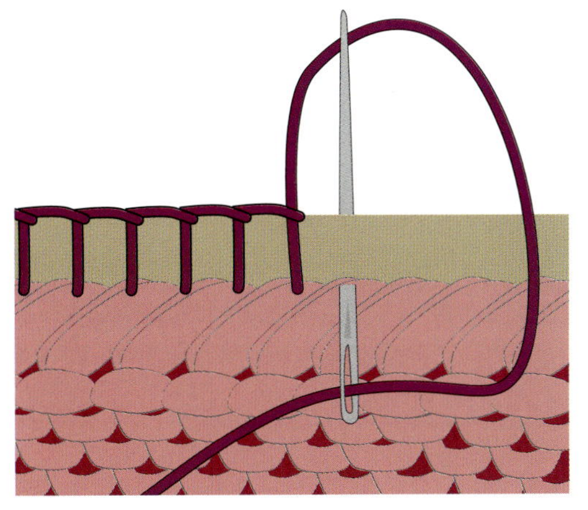

9 Stretch the cover over the lampshade and attach around the top and bottom edge using purple thread and blanket stitch (see page 17).

Chunky knit pouffe

Knitted pouffes are bang on trend at the moment. Make your own using macramé cord and your largest knitting loom!

YOU WILL NEED

- 165yds (150m) of 1/4in (6mm) 100% cotton macramé cord in natural
- 21in (53cm) diameter round loom, with 61 pegs set 3/4in (18mm) apart
- Knitting tool
- 1 x Dylon hand dye in each of French Lavender and Pewter Grey
- Salt
- Scissors
- Cream fleece fabric
- Sewing needle/machine and cream thread
- Stuffing

SIZE

- Approx. 10½in (26cm) diameter

INSTRUCTIONS

1 Begin by dyeing your cord. Mix the pack of lavender dye with a quarter of the Pewter Grey and salt, according to the instructions on the packet. Wrap your cord into loose hanks and dye/rinse according to the instructions. My cord has a marl effect, which is created when the dye doesn't get to all of the hank because it's more tightly tied. It's completely up to you what effect you go for. Once the cord is dried, you can begin knitting!

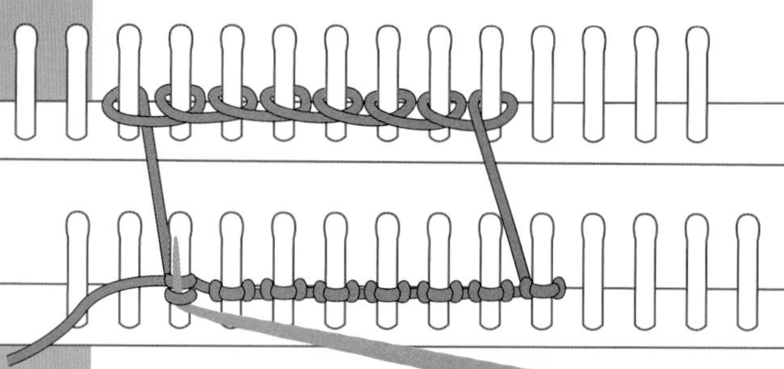

2 Cast on 16 stitches on the central part of the loom, using the e-wrap technique (see page 9). Knit for 3 rounds.

3 Increase by 4 stitches, by moving the end stitches out by one peg, moving all the stitches along by 2 pegs, then pick up the bar of the stitch below, twist, and place on the loom. You'll now have 20 stitches on the loom. Purl for 3 rounds.

4 Increase by 4 stitches again as in step 3, so there are now 24 stitches. Purl for 3 rounds.

5 Repeat steps 3 and 4 two more times, so there are now 32 stitches on the loom.

6 Repeat steps 3 and 4 again but increasing by 6 stitches four times evenly on the round, so there are 56 stitches on the loom.

7 Knit 3 rounds, purl 3 rounds, knit 3 rounds.

8 Now repeat steps 6 to 3 in reverse, but instead of increasing, knit 2 stitches together 6 times when you repeat step 6, and knit 2 stitches together 4 times when you repeat steps 5 to 3. As you decrease, move the stitches closer together again so there are no gaps.

9 Bind (cast) off using the gather method (see page 10).

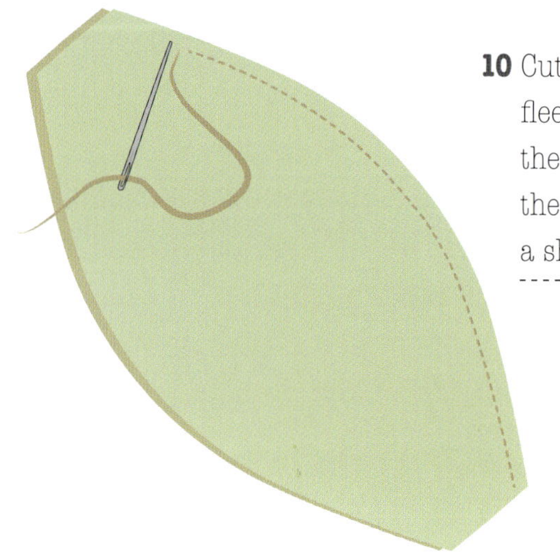

10 Cut 6 petal pieces from the fleece fabric and 2 circles, using the templates on page 123. Sew the "petals" together to make a shaped tube.

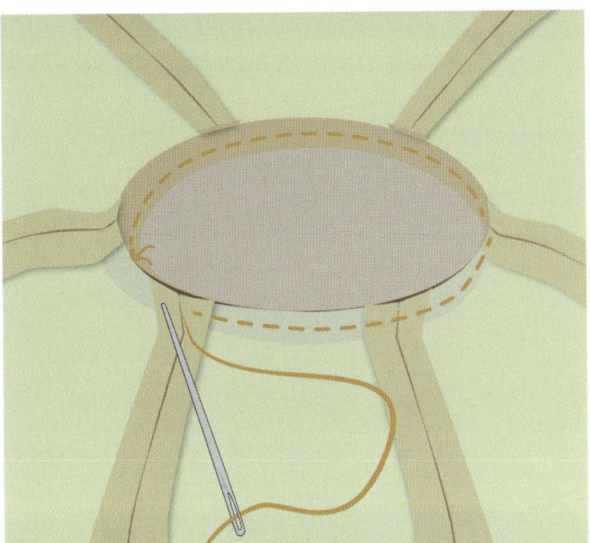

11 Sew one of the circles into the top of the tube of fabric.

12 Push the empty liner of fabric up inside the pouffe from the bottom. Fill the shell with stuffing. Sew the remaining circle of fleece into the open hole in the base of the fabric liner to complete.

Woven placemats

Another woven, rather than a knitted, project to get the most from your collection of looms! The ombré effect of this yarn looks fab in these quirky placemats. Try making matching coasters on a smaller loom.

YOU WILL NEED

- James C. Brett Party Time, 100% acrylic, bulky (chunky) yarn, 3½oz (100g) balls, approx. 168yds (154m) per ball: 1 ball of PT8
- 10½in (27cm) diameter round loom, with 41 pegs set ¾in (18mm) apart
- Knitting tool
- Scissors
- Tapestry needle
- Sewing machine and pink thread

SIZE

- Approx. 9¾in (24cm) diameter

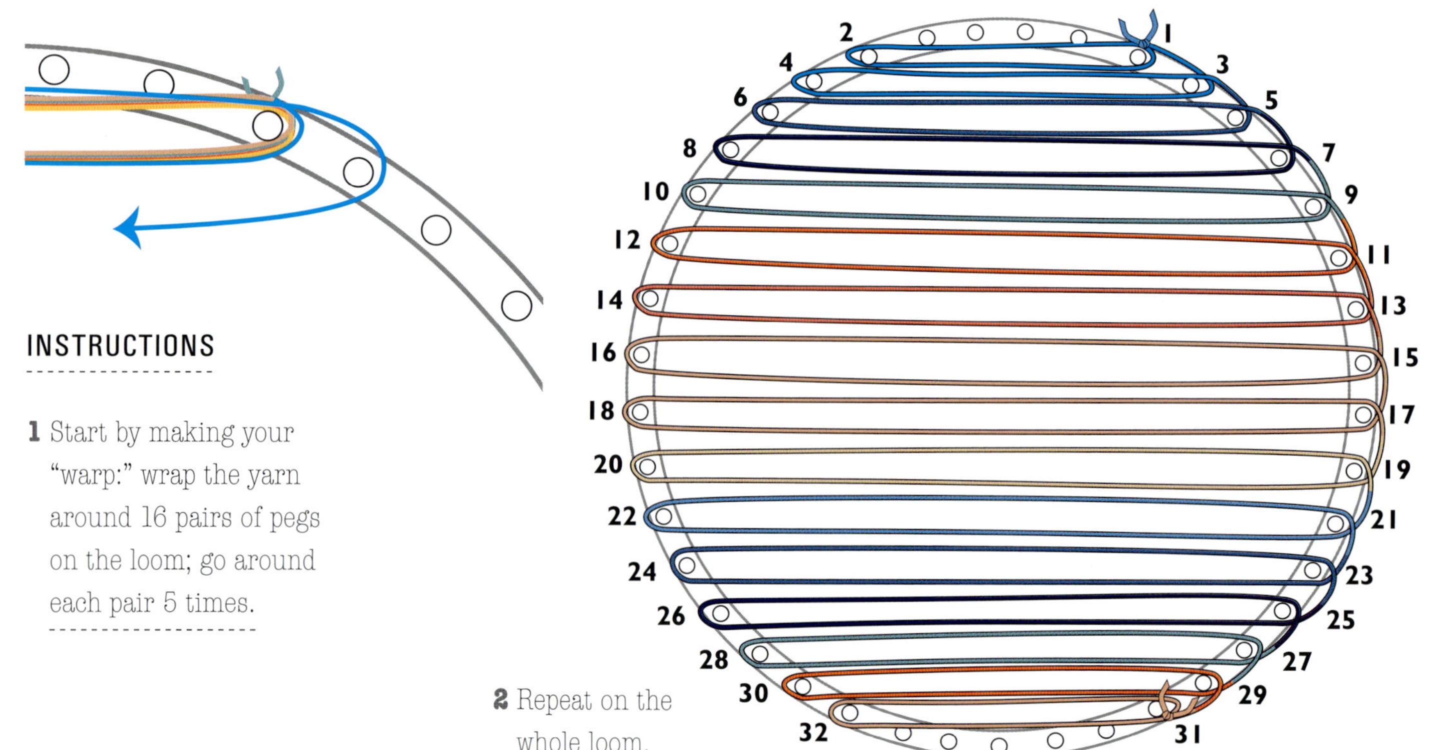

INSTRUCTIONS

1 Start by making your "warp:" wrap the yarn around 16 pairs of pegs on the loom; go around each pair 5 times.

2 Repeat on the whole loom.

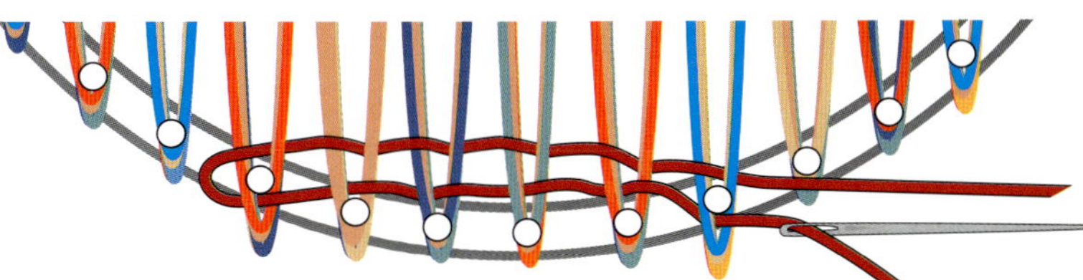

3 Cut a 60in (1.5m) piece of yarn and thread onto the tapestry needle. Turn the loom so that the warp is running vertically. Starting at the bottom, thread the yarn over and under the warp threads. Note that you start by going over the top of the pegs first and then come round below them. Repeat 5 times before moving onto the next pair of horizontal pegs.

4 Keep weaving backward and forward until the loom is full. Pull the fabric off the loom and, using the sewing machine, sew around the edge.

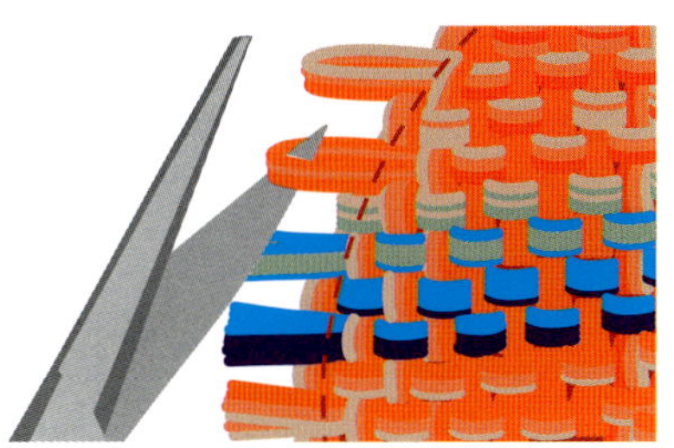

5 Trim the looped edges into a neat fringe.

6 Repeat to make further mats—one ball of yarn will make 2 mats.

Templates

All templates are printed at 100% and do not need to be enlarged. Use a photocopier or tracing paper and a pencil to copy a template, then cut out.

Fox storage jar

PAGE 110

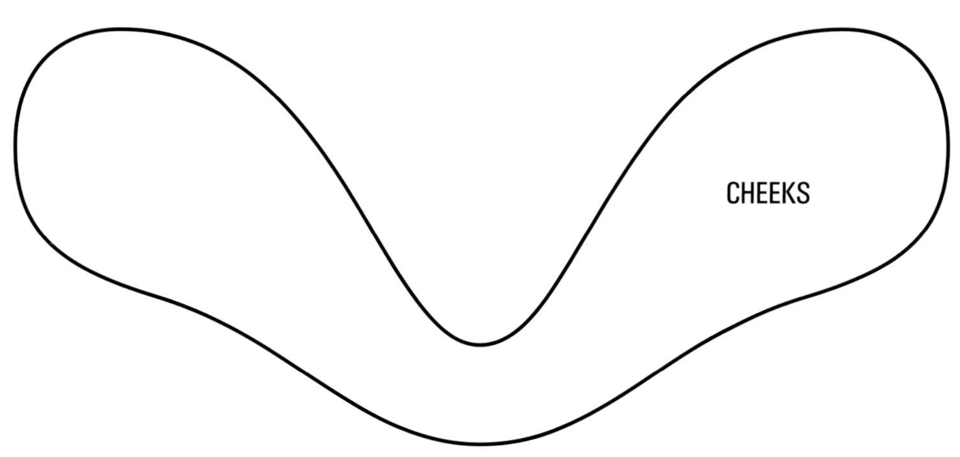

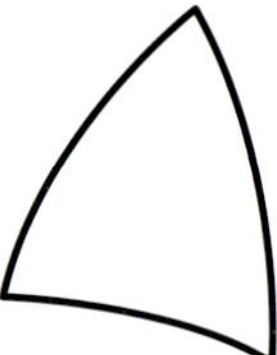

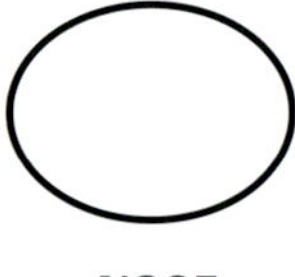

Chunky knit pouffe

PAGE 116

LINING PETAL—CUT 6

LINING CIRCLE—
CUT 2

Jungle finger puppets

PAGE 89

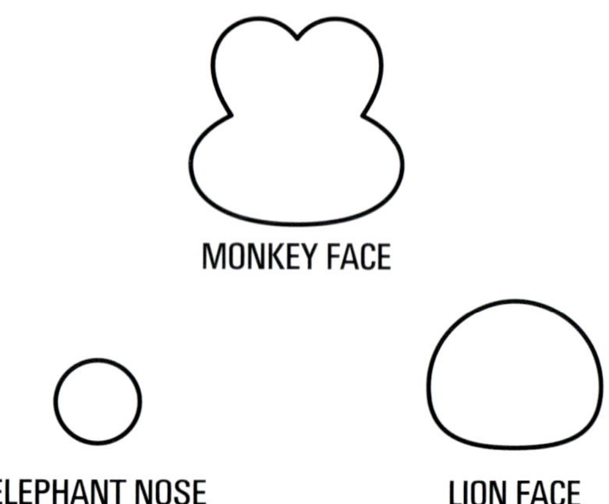

Japanese folded bag

PAGE 64

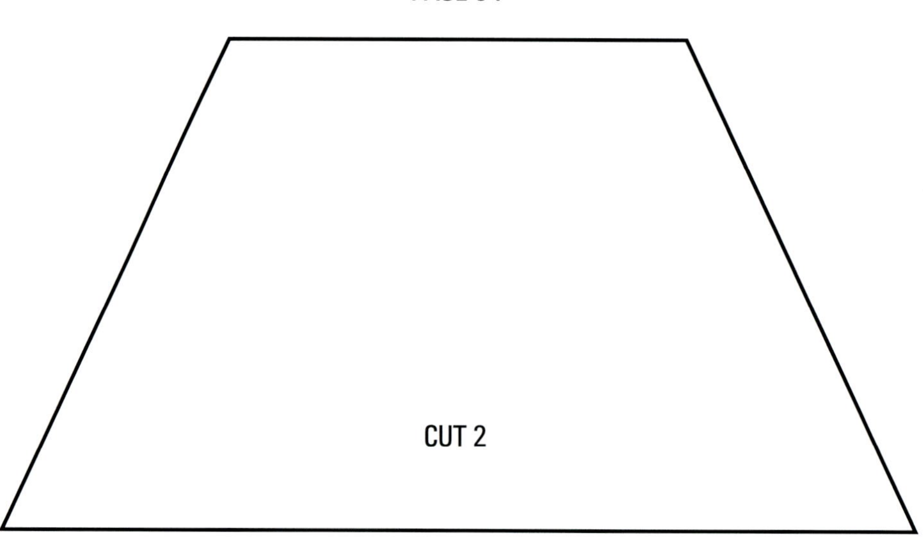

Suede and silk purse

PAGE 54

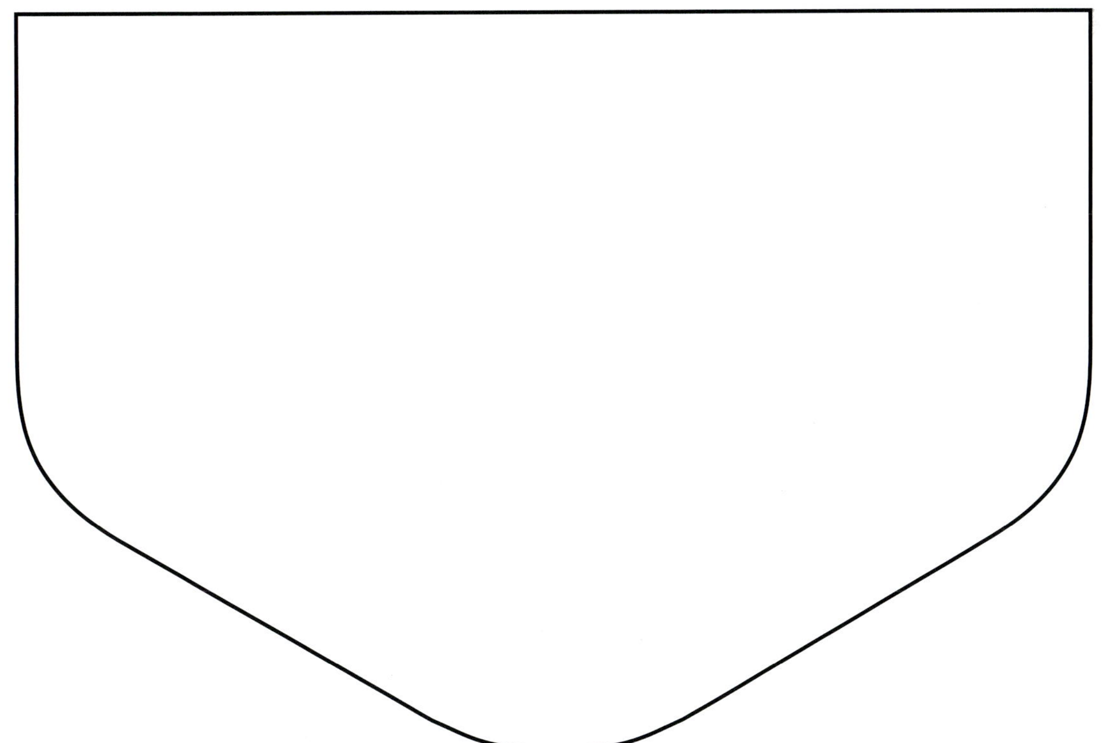

Resources

NORTH AMERICAN SUPPLIERS

Britex Fabrics
www.britexfabrics.com

Buyfabrics
www.buyfabrics.com

Hobby Lobby
www.hobbylobby.com

Knitting Fever
www.knittingfever.com

Michaels
www.michaels.com

Purl Soho
www.purlsoho.com

Sew Jersey
www.sewjersey.com

UK SUPPLIERS

Abakhan
www.abakhan.co.uk

Hobbycraft
www.hobbycraft.co.uk

John Lewis
www.johnlewis.com

LoveCrafts
www.lovecrafts.com

My Fabrics
www.myfabrics.co.uk

Wool Warehouse
www.woolwarehouse.co.uk

Index

Acknowledgments

Huge thanks must go to those at CICO, especially Penny Craig, for approaching me in the first place; also to in-house editor Anna Galkina, editor Marie Clayton, and illustrator Louise Turpin who worked closely with me on this gorgeous book. The photography and styling look fab as usual.

This would not have been possible without the help of my husband Jamie and mother-in-law, Sue, who helped look after our children during the production of this book so I could get knitting and writing.